The Proof is in the Pudding Cookbook

ISBN-13: 978-0-9846347-4-3
ISBN-10: 0-9846347-4-6

Originally printed in 2004

First ThomasMax printing, October 2011

Published by:

ThomasMax Publishing
P.O. Box 250054
Atlanta, GA 30325
www.thomasmax.com

tm

The Proof is in the Pudding Cookbook

*Featuring over 100 favorite recipes,
whimsical drawings, and
stories about cooking mishaps*

Evelyn Nalley McCollum
Illustrations by
Claire Gray Zeigler

ThomasMax

Your Publisher
For The 21st Century

This book contains recipes that I have collected during a lifetime of cooking. If you recognize one that you consider yours, my hope is that you will be flattered that it is included among my favorites.

-- *E.N.M.*

*Dedicated to the memory of my mother,
Mary Martitia Gray Nalley,
from whom I learned to cook by osmosis*

INTRODUCTION

I have many reasons for wanting to write a cookbook, or a book about cooking. I love to cook. I love to eat. I have lots of good recipes that I want to share. I want to share the knowledge I've gained in fifty years of cooking. I want to share hints and tips I've picked up. I want people to know how easy it is to cook.

When I was a child, I asked so many questions my family would get tired and refuse to answer me. Or they would tell me something so preposterous that I had to go off alone and think about what they had said. They accomplished their goal—to get me to stop asking questions—temporarily.

Nowhere is this inquisitiveness more maddening for me than in cooking—when I read instructions that I don't understand, or don't agree with. If I can't figure out a good reason, I'm likely not to follow the instructions. Sometimes I realize I should have; other times my method works as well, or better than the written instructions. That is one of the purposes in writing this cookbook. I want to tell you "why" and hopefully answer any questions ahead of time that might rise in your mind.

I grew up on family reunions and covered dish meals at church. I guess, because I was such a "quare" child during my early years, Mama fixed my plate with food she had brought. To this day, I can see that long table spread with all that delectable food, and here I am eating the same food I eat at home. Now when I go to a reunion, picnic or a covered dish meal, I try to get a bite of everything. Just a bite will do, but I have to try to taste everything I can see. When I eat something especially good, I keep asking around until I find the person who brought that particular food. Before I know it, I have another recipe to add to my collection.

I love it when I can't figure out what the ingredients are, or how the dish was made. My husband, Marion, and I went on a trip to the Holy Land with a group of people who were reluctant to eat anything they didn't recognize. Some of them actually got sick on the ten-day trip because they didn't eat enough. I remember one day at lunch we had something that looked like a meat patty with green things in it. Several members of our party wouldn't touch it. I assumed the green things were parsley, and if they were not, I'm trusting enough to believe that while I'm on a trip no one is going to put anything before that I shouldn't eat. On a trip to Hong Kong I realized, after I had already swallowed it, that I had just eaten a bird egg and that did make me feel a bit queasy.

I think I learned to cook by osmosis. Mama lived such a frugal existence that she was afraid my sisters or I would waste something, so rather than chance it, she did all the cooking at our house. But I spent so much time in the kitchen, watching her, that when I did begin to cook I knew instinctively what to do. After I married and had my own kitchen, I thoroughly enjoyed learning to cook by trial and error—and a lot of questions for Mama.

I look on cooking as an adventure, and I've found very few recipes that I couldn't improve. In fact, while reading a new recipe, I'm making mental notes as to how I will change it to make it better suit my taste buds. During my long years of cooking, I've tried many, many new recipes. If they didn't pass the test, they're not included in this book. What I have included are recipes that have become such favorites of our family that I want to share them. As a matter of fact, most of the recipes in this book are dishes that I cook over and over.

I challenge you to try my recipes and suggestions. I believe you will agree with me that cooking is not only easy, but also fun. I'm still learning, and experimenting, and thoroughly enjoying cooking. I hope you will, too.

I want to include a few notes of explanation: I have not yet learned to cook with fresh herbs and spices. When a recipe calls for a large amount of a fresh herb or spice, usually one teaspoon of dried spice is sufficient. Anyway, that's how I cook. The amount of food in cans keeps changing, so my numbers may not be entirely correct, but I think you get the idea of what size can to use.

This is a user-friendly book on cooking. I don't pretend to be an expert. I just want to share many of the recipes I've collected over the years, along with some humorous stories about mishaps along the way. I've made mistakes—that's part of the fun—to keep trying until I get it right, or as right as I can make it. Whether you're a seasoned cook or a beginner, my wish for you is that you dare to try something new, and have fun in the process.

The Bible says, "To everything there is a season, and a time to every purpose..." (Ecclesiastes 3:1). After working on this cookbook on and off for years, I feel that now is the time to complete it—coinciding with the premier showing of my play so that I can include the recipes of Annabel, Cornelia and Naomi. Another reason for choosing this particular time is that my granddaughter, Claire Gray Zeigler, can illustrate it. The publication just happens to coincide with Claire's first year at the Savannah College of Art and Design.

I've heard many women say they love to read cookbooks. If you're one of these women (or men), this cookbook is for you. Not only does it contain my best recipes, but also included are stories about many of these recipes. Once I mentioned to several women that I was working on a cookbook and told them a little about it. One woman said she would try the recipes but not read the stories. Another said she would read the stories but not try the recipes. My response was that there is something here for everyone.

CONTENTS

SALADS

Salmon Salad

Tuna Salad

Chicken Salad

Fruited Chicken Salad

Chicken or Turkey Salad

Turkey Salad

Holiday Turkey Salad

Black Bean Salad

Black Bean Pasta Salad

Bean Salad with Artichoke Hearts

White Bean and Tuna Salad

Corn and Pea Salad

Black-eyed Pea Salad

Sauer Kraut Salad

Broccoli Cauliflower Salad

Fruit Salad

Seven Layer Salad

Annabel's Prized Jell-O Salad

Jell-O Salads

SUMMER SALAD MEALS

Children are such finicky eaters. Not just my children—all children. Children don't like to eat combinations of food—they want to know exactly what they're eating. Some adults are like that, too. So while my children were home, I couldn't cook the casseroles, soups and salads that are now the mainstay of our diet. My cooking has done a complete turnaround from the time I was raising my family.

I don't have a favorite food. I love food—all food. I like individual foods and foods in combination—especially foods in combination. Because I am continually searching for and trying new recipes, I have found some great salads, both meat and vegetable, to serve during the hot summer months.

Another idiosyncrasy I have—which drives my adult children crazy--is that, though I live in the Deep South, I don't like air conditioning. I have to live in a closed up house all winter and I refuse to close my house up during the fall, spring and summer months. Therefore, we eat lots of salads in the summer.

Prepare a meat salad and a bean salad; add sliced tomatoes, cantaloupe and crackers and you have a good, nutritious summer meal. Even better, these salads can be made ahead so that at mealtime all you have to do is pull them out of the refrigerator. Another plus is that I usually have leftovers which are good for lunch.

When I became fat conscious, I stopped using mayonnaise and started experimenting. I find that Kraft Fat Free Salad Dressing with the red lid has a delicious taste and I now use it in everything that calls for mayonnaise.

Because salmon and cucumbers both have such distinct tastes, I'll have to admit that when I first read this recipe, I couldn't imagine them together, but this is a good salad. I used to pick the bones out of salmon until I learned how nutritious the bones are. Now I leave them in.

SALMON SALAD
1 can (8 ounce) salmon, drained
½ cup chopped cucumber
1 chopped green onion
1 tablespoon chopped pimento
Dash pepper
Mayonnaise to mix

Drain and flake salmon. Add other ingredients and mix well. Chill before serving. Since I don't know what to do with rest of a jar of pimento, I often leave it out or add chopped pepper instead. Or you could use the pimento in potato salad.

TUNA SALAD
1 can (6 ¼ ounce) tuna
1 stalk celery, chopped
1 tablespoon diced pickle
Mayonnaise to mix

This is a basic tuna salad. To make it more interesting, add one or all of the following: apple, pimento, green onions, nuts.

Traditionally our mothers made chicken salad to use up the rest of the hen they had cooked for Sunday dinner. Since not many of us cook hens that often anymore, the next best way is to cook a whole fryer and take the meat off the bones. (Save the broth and skim the fat before using.) Since I don't enjoy doing that, I've found the easiest way is to cook boneless chicken breasts and chop them. To give them more flavor, cook slowly in chicken broth, just enough to cover. You could, in an emergency, use canned chicken, but I don't like the taste of canned chicken.

CHICKEN SALAD
2 cups cooked chicken, chopped
1 cup chopped celery
½ cup chopped pickle
Mayonnaise

Mix well with mayonnaise. This is a basic chicken salad recipe. Listed below are variations.

FRUITED CHICKEN SALAD
2 cups cooked chicken, chopped
1 cup chopped celery
1 chopped green onion
½ teaspoon salt
2 tablespoons lemon juice
1 cup seedless grapes
1 can (11 ounce) Mandarin oranges, drained
½ cup slivered almonds
Mayonnaise to taste

Combine ingredient and mix well. (I chop the grapes in half.) Chill before serving.

I don't know when anyone cooks a turkey except at Thanksgiving and/or Christmas. These are good recipes to use that leftover turkey.

CHICKEN OR TURKEY SALAD
1 cup cooked chicken or turkey, chopped
1 tablespoon lemon juice
¼ cup chopped apple
½ cup chopped celery
2 tablespoons almonds
¼ teaspoon basil
Mayonnaise

Mix ingredients well and chill before serving.

TURKEY SALAD
1½ cups cooked turkey, chopped
1 cup celery, chopped
½ cup green grapes
Mayonnaise

Mix ingredients well and chill before serving.

HOLIDAY TURKEY SALAD
1 cup cooked turkey, chopped
½ cup chopped celery
½ cup pineapple tidbits
¼ cup almonds
Mayonnaise

Mix ingredients well and chill before serving.

I have always loved dried beans and in the past cooked them the old fashioned way. Since Mama did everything the hard way, it took me a long time to bring myself to buy canned beans, but I finally decided it is all right to use them.

BLACK BEAN SALAD
1 can (15½ ounce) black beans
½ red or green pepper, chopped
2 green onions, chopped
1 tablespoon fresh cilantro
1 tablespoon vinegar
1 teaspoon olive oil

Mix beans, pepper, green onions and cilantro. Mix vinegar and olive oil, pour over ingredients, and mix well. Chill before serving. You can substitute one teaspoon dried cilantro.

BLACK BEAN PASTA SALAD
8 ounces macaroni, cooked and drained
1½ tablespoons fresh lime juice
1½ teaspoons ground cumin
¼ teaspoon salt, or to taste
Freshly ground black pepper to taste
4 green onions, trimmed and sliced
1 can (15 ½ ounce) black beans, rinsed and drained
2 tablespoons chopped fresh cilantro

Prepare macaroni according to package directions. Mix lime juice, cumin, salt and pepper. Toss with macaroni, onions, beans, and cilantro. Chill before serving. As you might have suspected, I don't keep lime juice on hand so I substitute lemon. I'm sure lime is better.

Because this salad is so filling and almost a meal in itself, it probably should be in the entrée section. I serve this salad in the summer with sliced tomato, cantaloupe and crackers.

BEAN SALAD WITH ARTICHOKE HEARTS
1 cup chopped tomato
½ cup red bell pepper, chopped
½ cup red onion, chopped
¼ cup fresh parsley, chopped
1 can (19 ounce) chickpeas, drained
1 can (19 ounce) red kidney beans, drained
1 can (14 ounce) quartered artichoke hearts, drained

DRESSING
2 tablespoons fresh lemon juice
1 tablespoon olive oil
1 tablespoon balsamic vinegar
1½ teaspoons spicy brown mustard
1 teaspoon dried basil
1 teaspoon dried oregano
1 teaspoon dried thyme
1 clove garlic, minced
¼ cup Feta cheese, crumbled

Mix the seven salad ingredients together. Combine the next eight ingredients in a small bowl, stirring with a whisk. Pour dressing over the salad. Sprinkle Feta cheese on top. Cover and chill at least one hour before serving.

Here is another salad that is a meal in itself, served with crackers, sliced tomatoes and cantaloupe, or with fruit. The recipe I found called for cannelloni beans but since I can never find them, I substitute white soup beans. The solid white tuna is worth the differences in price compared to the cheaper varieties.

WHITE BEAN AND TUNA SALAD
2 tablespoons fresh lemon juice
1 tablespoon olive oil
¼ teaspoon salt
½ teaspoon pepper
½ teaspoon oregano
1 can (20 ounce) white beans, drained
1 can (6 ½ ounce) solid white tuna, drained
4 green onions, chopped
2 tablespoons fresh parsley

Mix first five ingredients together. Toss dressing with beans, tuna and onions. Sprinkle parsley on top. Chill before serving.

I've noticed that my family doesn't like this salad as well as I do, but it's a marvelous color combination—green peas, carrots and corn. When I can't figure out which vegetable or salad to use, I pull out this recipe. I usually have lots of it left over, but no matter. It keeps well, so I eat it for lunch until it's gone.

CORN AND PEA SALAD
1 can (12 ounce) white shoepeg corn, drained
1 can (16 ounce) green peas, drained
1 medium carrot, grated
2 tablespoons chopped onion
¼ teaspoon oregano
1/8 teaspoon black pepper
1 tablespoon rice vinegar

Mix the ingredients together. Chill before serving. Green onions can be substituted as well as yellow corn. I usually add mayonnaise to the mixture. You can serve it either way.

In addition to my discovering canned dried beans, I found all these delicious canned peas—at least four varieties—and all

I have to do is open a can and heat them, or serve them cold in salads. In the recipe below, green pepper works just as well as red. I use canned mushrooms but you may prefer fresh.

BLACK-EYED PEA SALAD
1 can (15 ounce) black-eyed peas, drained
1 can (15 ounce) whole kernel corn, drained
1 cup diced carrot
1 cup diced celery
1 cup diced red pepper
½ cup thinly sliced fresh mushrooms
2 tablespoons minced red onion
¼ cup rice vinegar
½ cup chopped cilantro leaves
Salt and pepper to taste

Combine vegetables in a large bowl; pour vinegar over and toss. Chill. Thirty minutes before serving add cilantro and toss. If fresh cilantro is not available, substitute one teaspoon dried cilantro. Season with salt and pepper.

Next are two salads that are good to take to picnics and covered dish meals, or on hayrides, because they can be made ahead, and they are big dishes that serve ten to twelve.

SAUER KRAUT SALAD
1/3 cup oil
¾ cup vinegar
1¾ cups sugar
2 cans (16 ounce) sauer kraut, drained
1 small can (8 ounce) water chestnuts
1 small jar (4 ounce) pimento
3 stalks celery, chopped
1 onion, chopped

Mix oil, vinegar, and sugar and bring to a boil. Mix next five ingredients and pour dressing over. I prefer chopped kraut over shredded. I slice the water chestnuts into smaller pieces. The longer this mixture sits in the refrigerator the sweeter and better tasting it gets.

BROCCOLI CAULIFLOWER SALAD
1 large bunch broccoli, chopped
1 small cauliflower, chopped
1 small red onion, chopped
2 large stalks celery, chopped
Mushrooms, fresh or canned
Slivered almonds
Ranch salad dressing

Mix all ingredients with dressing; refrigerate several hours or overnight before serving. The longer this salad sits, the better it gets. Any of the bottled Ranch salad dressings, fat-free or regular, will do, but the original dry packet mixed with mayonnaise and buttermilk is wonderful. Use non-fat buttermilk and non-fat or low-fat mayonnaise to cut the fat and calories.

Because it is so easy to prepare, often I take this fruit salad to covered dish meals. I like to watch the facial expression of someone who is eating it for the first time. He (or she) will take a bite, look puzzled, and invariably look to the person closest to them and ask, "What is this?"

"This" is the combination of Tang and instant pudding, which makes a delicious fruit salad dressing with an unusual taste.

When I give this recipe to friends and family, some of them can't seem to get it right. Pay close to attention to the caution at the end of the recipe.

FRUIT SALAD
1 can (16 ounce) chunky mixed fruit
1 can (15 ½ ounce) pineapple chunks
3 tablespoons orange Tang
1 small package vanilla instant pudding and pie filling
1 can (6 ounce) mandarin oranges
2 large bananas, sliced
Maraschino cherries

Drain **mixed fruit** and discard juice; slice fruit into bite sized pieces. Drain pineapple and **save juice**. Combine pineapple juice and Tang, stir until dissolved. Add dry pudding and mix well. Combine chunky fruit, pineapple and mandarin oranges with dressing; toss gently. Chill. Just before serving, add sliced bananas and dot the top with well-drained red maraschino cherries. I've also tried lemon pudding mix with good results.

Caution: Don't mix the instant pudding with milk. Mix the dry powder with the fruit juice. Be sure to use instant pudding, not the kind that has to be cooked.

When I became fat conscious and stopped eating mayonnaise I stopped making this salad, but now that I have discovered fat-free salad dressing, it has come back into my good graces. You could also use reduced fat mayonnaise.

SEVEN LAYER SALAD
1 head lettuce, torn in pieces
1 small onion, chopped, or green onions
2 stalks celery, chopped
1 can or package (16 ounce) frozen English peas
6 ounces grated cheddar cheese
1 cup mayonnaise
Bacon bits

Tear lettuce by hand (lettuce cut with a knife turns brown) and put in large bowl. Add onion and celery. Add peas. Frozen peas don't have to be cooked, but they should be thawed. Spread mayonnaise on top like icing on a cake. Sprinkle cheese on top of mayonnaise. Sprinkle bacon bits on top. The last time I made this salad my main dish contained several types of cheese so I substituted grated carrots for the grated cheese with good results.

ANNABEL'S PRIZED JELL-O SALAD

1 package (3 ounce) lime gelatin
1 can (8 ounce) crushed pineapple
1 package (3 ounce) lemon gelatin
1 package (8 ounce) cream cheese, softened
1 cup chopped pecans
1 package (3 ounce) strawberry gelatin
1 can (14 ½ ounce) fruit cocktail
Whipped topping

Dissolve lime gelatin in one cup boiling water. Stir in crushed pineapple. Pour into 12 x 7½ x 2 dish. Chill until firm.

Mix lemon gelatin with two cups boiling water. Stir in softened cream cheese and nuts. Spread over first layer. Chill until firm.

Mix strawberry gelatin with one cup boiling water. Stir in fruit cocktail. Pour over top and chill again. When dish has set completely, cover with whipped topping.

Is it any wonder that Annabel got upset with Wesley when he ruined her dish that she had spent so much time on?

o ANNABEL o

JELL-O SALADS

I was always amazed that my family liked Jell-O and fruit so much. I believe they would have eaten any combination I put before them. When I use canned fruit, I don't drain the fruit and reduce the water accordingly. Listed below are some of our favorites.

STRAWBERRY—Add fresh or frozen strawberries to strawberry Jell-O. Or use strawberry banana Jell-O and add sliced bananas along with the strawberries.

BLUEBERRY SALAD--Add one small can (8 ounce) crushed pineapple and 1 can (15 ounce) blueberries (drained) to two small packages black cherry Jell-O. Use fresh blueberries if available.

PINEAPPLE ORANGE SALAD--Add one small can (8 ounce) crushed pineapple and one small can (8 ounce) mandarin oranges to two small packages orange Jell-O. Sometimes I drain canned fruit and sometimes I don't. I always feel like I am discarding vitamins and minerals when I drain anything.

FRUIT COCKTAIL SALAD--Add one can (16 ounce) fruit cocktail to one box of strawberry, cherry, or raspberry Jell-O, or two cans to any combination of two flavors. This was the old standby that Mama made all the time when I was a child, and she didn't drain the fruit cocktail. Mama didn't drain *anything.*

CHERRY JELL-O--Add one can (16 ounce) tart cherries to one box of cherry Jell-O. You may want to add ¼ or ½ cup sugar. I don't drain these cherries.

SOUPS

Vegetable Soup

Shrimp, Kale and Chickpea Soup

Taco Soup

Peasant Soup

Mexican Chicken Soup

Seafood Gumbo

Cuban Black Bean Soup

Brown Rice and Lentil Soup

Chili and Beans

OUR FAVORITE SOUPS

After our children left home, my cooking habits changed drastically, and I started making a lot of one-dish meals. When discussing my empty nest with a friend, she said they ate a lot of soup. That seemed like a good idea, so I started trying different kinds of canned soup. These soups were okay, but they didn't really measure up to my expectations of a good meal. Canned soup tastes like canned soup. When I started reading labels and realized how much salt and fat these soups contain, I started experimenting with various kinds of homemade soup.

After reading many soup recipes and trying different ones, I came up with these which have become our favorites. I make the full recipe (it's impossible to make a small amount of soup, so I don't even try), then freeze the leftovers in one and one-half pint containers; this makes two good servings. A one-quart crockpot is perfect for warming soup for two people.

In the early fall, when there's a nip in the air, I begin making soup. By the time I have made all of them, I have quite a supply in the freezer which takes us through most of the winter. It's wonderful to come from work, or a day's shopping, or from doing volunteer work, to find a nutritious, hot soup waiting to be enjoyed.

The first recipe is my basic vegetable soup. If I have left over beef, chicken, ham, or pork, I add it to the soup. I used to think I couldn't make soup without adding beef (Mama always made it that way), but I've discovered that vegetable soup without any kind of meat is delicious.

Most of the time I cook fresh carrots instead of using canned. The reason I buy individual canned or frozen vegetables instead of using mixed vegetables is because all mixed vegetable packages contain green beans. Though green beans are one of my favorite vegetables, I don't want them in soup. I've tried picking them out, but it's not worth the effort.

I've tried canned and frozen okra, and frozen is better. If you have access to okra and/or vine ripened tomatoes during the growing season which you can or freeze, by all means use them.

Diced potatoes can be added if you don't plan to freeze the soup; potatoes don't freeze well. To make heartier soup, try adding rice or cooked barley. Rice will cook along with the soup but barley needs to be cooked separately. Once I made soup with barley and I kept getting these little hard pellets in my mouth. Though I had kept the soup warm for ages, it never got hot enough to cook the barley.

Listed below are the ingredients I usually use when making vegetable soup. Cooking is subjective, and soup is probably the most subjective dish there is. Experiment and substitute until you find the vegetable soup perfect for you and your family.

I use equal amounts of the ingredients listed—a tall can, or ten ounce box or one pound bag of frozen vegetables. Please forgive me for my discrepancies in listing the size of cans in these recipes. Some are 16 ounce, some 15 and some 14 ½, but I think you know which size I am referring to.

VEGETABLE SOUP
1 can or package frozen kernel corn
1 can or package frozen lima beans
1 can or package frozen English peas
1 can or package frozen carrots
1 can or package frozen okra
2 cans tomatoes
1 can tomato soup

Mix ingredients together in a crockpot. Cook at least 8 hours. If you prefer to cook in a pot on the stove, cook until heated through. Vegetable soup is a matter of taste; I like mine thick. If you want thinner soup, add one can (14 ½ ounce) beef, chicken or vegetable broth. Water weakens the flavor of soup.

When I read this recipe I thought, shrimp, kale and chickpeas? But since I'm game to try anything once, I tried this mixture and found it to be delicious. Adding greens to soup is new to me, and I wonder why I didn't know about it sooner. The recipe calls for one-half package of greens, but what's a few more ounces of greens going to hurt in this much soup? Besides, what can you do with five ounces of greens?

SHRIMP, KALE AND CHICKPEA SOUP
1 tablespoon olive oil
2 medium onions, chopped
2 large carrots, thinly sliced
1 stalk celery, chopped
3-4 cloves garlic, minced
¼ teaspoon black pepper
2 cans (14½ ounce) chicken broth
2 cans (15 ounce) chickpeas, drained
1 can (14 ounce) stewed tomatoes
½ of a 10 ounce package frozen
chopped kale or collard greens
½ teaspoon ground coriander
½ teaspoon turmeric
¼ teaspoon pepper
8 ounces raw shrimp

Sauté onions, carrots, celery, garlic, pepper and a pinch of salt in the oil for 7-10 minutes. Add everything else except the shrimp. Cover and bring mixture to a boil. Reduce heat to low and simmer 15 minutes. Stir in shrimp, cover and simmer 2-3 minutes until shrimp are pink. This recipe can be made in a crockpot, adding shrimp a few minutes before serving.

Listed below is one of those rare recipes that I can't improve. The only thing I can even remotely think of to make this soup better is to add two cans of corn rather than one. In my weekly column for *The Easley Progress,* I sometimes share recipes. Judging from the response I got from readers, I believe Taco Soup became their favorite.

TACO SOUP
2 pounds ground turkey or beef (I always use beef)
1 medium onion chopped
1 envelope Taco seasoning
1 regular envelope ranch salad dressing mix
1 can (10½ ounce) tomatoes with chilies (Ro-tel)
2 cans (14 ½ ounce) tomatoes, crushed or diced
1 can (15½ ounce) pinto beans, drained
1 can (15½ ounce) red kidney beans, drained
1 can (12 ½ ounce) white corn

Cook meat in water until pink is gone. Drain water. Add onion and cook until tender. Stir the two dry mixes into the browned meat and onions. Add tomatoes, beans and corn. Heat to serving temperature and enjoy.

I think the reason I like this soup so much is that Mama used to stew potatoes with lots of butter. When she served the piping hot potatoes, we mashed them up with the broth and ate them with fresh-baked cornbread. Delicious! This, too, sounds like a strange combination but trust me, I think you'll like it.

For a long time I avoided soup recipes that called for potatoes since I didn't want to freeze soup containing potatoes but I finally figured out the way to do it. I make the soup recipe, without the potatoes, take out the amount I want to serve immediately and add potatoes to that portion. I freeze the rest of the soup in two-serving size containers. I write "add potatoes" on the label so I will know to add potatoes the next time around.

PEASANT SOUP

2 medium carrots, chopped
1 large onion, chopped
2 celery ribs, sliced
1 tablespoon oil
¼ cup chopped parsley
16 ounces Kielbasa sausage, chopped
1 bay leaf
3 cans (15 ounce) chicken broth
10 ounces cabbage, chopped
2 russet potatoes, cut into cubes
2 cans (15 ounce) red kidney beans, drained
¼ teaspoon thyme
½ teaspoon pepper

Cook carrots, onions and celery in oil until tender. Add remaining ingredients. Bring to a boil then simmer until time to serve.

This recipe is similar to Taco Soup, but it calls for chicken instead of ground beef and black beans instead of pinto.

MEXICAN CHICKEN SOUP
2 chicken breasts
1 large onion, chopped
1 tablespoon oil
2 cans (15 ounce) tomatoes
1 can (10 ½ ounce) Ro-tel Mexican tomatoes
1 can (15 ounce) red kidney beans, drained
1 can (15 ounce) black beans, drained
1 can (15 ounce) whole kernel corn
2 cans (16 ounce) chicken broth
1½ teaspoons chili powder
1 teaspoon sugar
½ teaspoon salt
1 teaspoon cilantro

Cook the chicken breasts and chop into small pieces. Sauté onion in oil. Add tomatoes, beans, broth, and spices. Bring to a boil and simmer for about 30 minutes. The longer you cook this soup—or any soup—the tastier it becomes.

After trying gumbo in both New Orleans and Hilton Head, I came up with this recipe for seafood gumbo. You can serve gumbo over rice, but we prefer to eat gumbo as soup. If you feel energetic, you can chop onion, celery and bell pepper and add to the gumbo instead of Ro-tel tomatoes. If you have home frozen okra and home canned tomatoes, this gumbo is out of sight.

SEAFOOD GUMBO
1 package (16 ounce) frozen okra (thawed)
4 cans (14 ½ ounce) tomatoes
1 can (10 ½ ounce) Ro-tel tomatoes
Polish sausage to taste
1 pound thawed, cleaned, deveined shrimp

Place okra and tomatoes and Polish sausage in the crock-pot. Cook overnight if you plan to have gumbo for lunch the next day. Start it early in the morning if you want it for dinner. Add the shrimp the last 15 minutes or so. I believe shrimp would disappear if you cooked it long enough. If the shrimp is large, cut it in two or three pieces.

Our family has just recently discovered black beans, and I like them in both soups and salads. Sometimes I leave out the orange juice; I don't see that it adds that much flavor.

CUBAN BLACK BEAN SOUP
1 cup chopped onion
2 cloves garlic
1 teaspoon cumin
1 teaspoon coriander
1 teaspoon paprika
3 tablespoons olive oil
1 cup chopped carrots
1 medium green pepper
Black pepper
1/4 cup chopped fresh parsley
1 cup orange juice
1 can (14½ ounce) tomatoes
4 cans (14½ ounce) drained black beans
1 can (10 ½ ounce) Ro-tel tomatoes (optional)

Cook onions and garlic in olive oil. Add other ingredients. Cook until heated through. To simplify this recipe, you can use garlic in a jar, or dried garlic. Dried parsley, one tablespoon, can be substituted for fresh. Fresh tomatoes can be substituted and cooked dried beans can be substituted for canned. Just to make the dish more interesting, I add one can of Ro-tel tomatoes.

We've also just discovered lentils and this soup is good for a change of pace from vegetables and beans.

BROWN RICE AND LENTIL SOUP
1½ cups diced carrots
1 cup chopped onion
½ cup chopped celery
1 cup sliced mushrooms
3 cloves garlic
2 cans (16 ounce) chicken or vegetable stock
1 (14 ½ ounce) can chopped tomatoes
1½ cup red lentils
1 cup uncooked brown rice
1½ teaspoons dried basil
1½ teaspoons dried thyme
1½ teaspoons dried oregano
½ teaspoon dried hot red pepper flakes
2 bay leaves
½ cup chopped parsley
Salt and pepper to taste

In a large kettle, combine vegetables, stock, tomatoes, lentils, rice and herbs, except for the parsley. Bring to a boil and simmer, stirring occasionally, for about 35 minutes or until the lentils and rice are tender. Season with salt and pepper, remove the bay leaves, add parsley and serve.

NOTE: Not all brown rice will cook in 35 minutes. Check the package direction on the rice you are using. You may have to adjust the cooking time or cook the rice separately before adding to the soup.

An old standby one-dish meal is Chili and Beans. Once my older son came home from college unexpectedly and brought his current girl friend. For supper I had prepared a crockpot full of chili and beans. I didn't remember his particularly liking chili and beans while he was at home, and was a bit miffed that he did not let me know he was coming, and embarrassed that I had nothing better to offer. However, they ate the chili and beans like this was the best meal they'd ever had. I don't think they would have enjoyed a steak more. Again, I read several recipes and came up with my own.

CHILI AND BEANS
1 pound ground chuck
1 onion, chopped
1 tablespoon chili powder
1 teaspoon salt
¼ teaspoon pepper
1 can (15 ounce) light red kidney beans
1 can (15 ounce) dark red kidney beans
1 can (15 ounces) pinto beans
2 cans (15 ounce) tomatoes
1 can (8 ounce) tomato sauce
1 can (10½ ounce) Ro-tel tomatoes

Brown ground beef; drain. Cook onion. Add chili powder, salt and pepper. Drain beans. Add with tomatoes. Cook until heated through. This is one of those recipes that can simmer a long time, or you can eat it as soon as it gets hot. It freezes well.

MAIN DISHES

Baked Stew

Barbecued Meat Loaf

Beef Roast

Nacho Skillet Dinner

Parmesan Chicken Fingers

Ham Crescents

Oven Baked Tenderloin

Basic Marinades

Barbecue Sauce

Barbecued Ribs

Barbecued Chicken

Tuna Casserole

Baked Catfish

Salmon Croquettes

New Salmon Croquettes

Salmon Crabmeat Patties

GOOD MEALS DON'T HAVE TO BE EXPENSIVE

The recipes listed below call for inexpensive meats such as ground beef, tuna and canned salmon. Maybe these recipes are a holdover from the days when I had a growing family and had to stretch the food dollar to its limit, but these recipes have remained favorites through the years. I'm also sharing recipes for pork, chicken, beef and ham which can be bought at sale prices. You may need to splurge a little to buy pork tenderloin.

We've all cooked stew beef on the stove or in a crockpot, but here's a new twist to an old recipe that is even easier to prepare and delicious to eat.

BAKED STEW

2 pounds stew beef
2 cups onion
2 cups potatoes, cubed
2 cups carrots, sliced
2 cups celery, chopped
1 can (8 ounce) sliced mushrooms
1 teaspoon salt
½ teaspoon pepper
1 teaspoon sugar
1 can (46 ounce) V-8 vegetable juice
5 tablespoons tapioca (or flour)

Place first six ingredients in a roaster pan with a tight fitting lid. Mix salt, pepper and sugar and sprinkle over meat and vegetables. Pour V-8 over all. Sprinkle tapioca or flour over mixture. Bake at 250 degrees five to seven hours.

People look as if they don't believe me when I tell them that meat loaf is one of my boys' favorites, but I continue to make this dish when we are all together, such as on our yearly vacation at the beach. The secret to the meatloaf is the sauce on top. These same people do a double take when I tell them the name of the recipe is Barbecued Meat Loaf.

BARBECUED MEAT LOAF
1 slice of bread or ½ cup bread crumbs
½ cup milk, canned, whole, or skim
1 can (8 ounce) tomato sauce
1 egg
Salt and pepper
1 to 1½ pounds ground beef
1 small onion, chopped
½ small bell pepper, chopped

Place bread in large bowl, pour milk and about one-fourth of the can of tomato sauce over to soften. Add egg, and salt and pepper. Mix. Add half of meat; mix. Add rest of meat, onion and bell pepper. Mix well. Put in one-quart oven dish. Cook at 350 degrees for thirty minutes.

BARBECUE SAUCE
2 tablespoons brown sugar
2 tablespoons vinegar
1 tablespoon Worcestershire Sauce
Pinch of dry mustard

Add brown sugar, vinegar, Worcestershire sauce and mustard to the remaining tomato sauce in the can, mix well and set aside. Cook meat loaf for 30 minutes. Take out of oven and pour off fat. Pour barbecue sauce on top of meat loaf. Cook 30 minutes more. Let cool slightly before cutting into squares.

I guess because Mama never cooked that way, I've never been comfortable cooking a beef roast in the oven unless I either cover it with foil or put a lid on it. I'm always afraid it will dry out. Nothing could be simpler than cooking a roast in a crockpot. It always comes out moist and tasty—I consider this a foolproof way to cook a roast.

BEEF ROAST

Rub roast with salt and pepper. Brown in frying pan on all sides. Place in crockpot; cook on low at least eight hours. Take roast from crockpot. Pour broth into container. Skim fat off top. To make gravy, I use two tablespoons cornstarch to one and one-half cups broth. If you like your gravy thicker or thinner, use more or less cornstarch. Mix cornstarch with a small amount of water, stir until dissolved, add to COLD broth. Cook over medium heat, stirring constantly, until thick. Some recipes say to beat with a whisk while the gravy is cooking. If you use cold, or warm broth, the cornstarch mixture won't lump when you add it.

If you have a yearning for something Mexican, this is a quick and easy dish to prepare. I love the combination of meat, beans, tomato, corn and cheese.

NACHO SKILLET DINNER
1 pound ground beef
1 can (15½ ounce) red kidney beans, drained
1 can (15½ ounce) kernel corn
1 can (8 ounce) tomato sauce
1 jar (16 ounce) salsa
1 teaspoon garlic powder
1 teaspoon chili powder
1 cup shredded Cheddar cheese
Nacho chips

Brown ground beef, stirring constantly. Pour off fat. Add beans, tomato sauce, salsa, garlic powder and chili powder. Heat through. Cover and let simmer. Top with grated cheese on serving plate. Serve chips on the side. This can also be served as a thick soup.

Fried chicken fingers have become a staple these days, but chicken fingers can also be baked. In addition to being delicious, these fingers are easy to prepare, and you don't have to deal with deep frying them, not to mention the fat you're not putting into your body.

PARMESAN CHICKEN FINGERS
8 boneless, skinless chicken breasts
2 cups dry breadcrumbs
¾ cup Parmesan cheese
½ teaspoon salt
½ teaspoon pepper
2 garlic cloves, chopped
1 cup butter or margarine, melted

Cut each chicken breast into three or four strips. In large bowl, combine breadcrumbs, cheese, salt and pepper. Sauté garlic in butter or margarine; remove from heat. Add chicken and let sit three minutes. Roll chicken in breadcrumb mixture and place in 13 x 9 baking dish. Bake at 400 degrees 10 to 12 minutes. These chicken fingers are delicious served warm or cold, and are perfect for a tailgate party.

I discovered this recipe while browsing through a magazine. This is one of my favorite pastimes, reading recipes and trying new ones. New recipes don't always become keepers. Many times I try a recipe once and once is enough.

But this recipe, which we renamed Ham Crescents, has become one of my preferred ways for using leftover ham. In fact, when I buy a ham, I also buy crescent rolls and a three-ounce package of cream cheese so I'll have ingredients on hand for the follow-up meal.

HAM CRESCENTS
1 package (3 ounce) cream cheese
2 tablespoons butter or margarine
2 tablespoons milk
2 cups chopped ham
2 tablespoons chopped onion
1 jar (2 ounce) pimento
1 package (8 ounce) crescent rolls

Put cream cheese, butter and milk in a plastic container and microwave for about one minute; this makes the cream cheese and butter much easier to mix. Add ham, onion and pimento, mix well. Separate crescent rolls into four squares, sealing perforations. Spoon one-fourth mixture on each square. Bring corners together in the center, covering the filling. Pinch seams together to seal. Place on an ungreased cookie sheet and bake at 350 degrees 20 to 25 minutes, or until golden brown.

In the olden days pork tenderloin was considered a delicacy. We fried it and ate it with eggs and grits for breakfast, or as a breakfast meal at night. Now pork tenderloin is considered a staple and this baked tenderloin has a unique flavor that my family enjoys.

OVEN BAKED PORK TENDERLOIN
2 (3/4 pounds each) pork tenderloins
½ cup butter or margarine
½ cup soy sauce
½ teaspoon cumin
¼ teaspoon ginger
¼ teaspoon coriander
¼ teaspoon Tabasco

1 tablespoon lemon juice
2 cloves garlic, minced

Melt butter; add spices in glass baking dish. Place tenderloin in baking dish. Turn tenderloins so that they are coated on all sides. Bake at 325 degrees, uncovered, 1½ hours or until meat thermometer registers 160 degrees.

Below are two marinades that I use on pork chops and boneless chicken breast.

BASIC MARINADE NO. 1
2 tablespoons soy sauce
2 tablespoons sherry
2 tablespoons oil
1 teaspoon ginger

or

MARINADE NO. 2
¼ cup soy sauce
2 tablespoons sherry
1 teaspoon oil
1 teaspoon sugar
1 teaspoon ginger
1 teaspoon garlic powder

Mix ingredients together. Place chicken or pork chops in shallow pan with lid or in a zip-lock bag. Turn once or twice. I marinate the meat for several hours, or overnight. Take meat out of marinade and grill until done.

I have a basic barbecue sauce that I use with everything I want to barbecue. I altered the original recipe extensively, leaving out the water and oil which do nothing but make the sauce thin and full of fat.

This sauce is wonderful on any kind of pork and especially pork ribs; it is also good on chicken. On a snow day recently I made this recipe, increasing all the ingredients by a third, and put it in a squeeze catsup bottle. Now I have the barbecue sauce at my fingertips. It will keep indefinitely stored in the refrigerator.

In this recipe, you may notice that I listed the dry ingredients first. That way my measuring spoon stays dry until I finish measuring dry ingredients. You may think this is picky-picky, but it's one of those little details that makes cooking easier for me.

BARBECUE SAUCE
6 tablespoons brown sugar
2 teaspoons dry mustard
2 teaspoons chili powder
2 teaspoons paprika
1 teaspoon red pepper
1 teaspoon salt
2 teaspoons lemon juice
6 tablespoons vinegar
4 tablespoons Worcestershire sauce
6 tablespoons catsup

Mix ingredients together. Store in refrigerator. Use on pork or chicken. You may want to decrease the amount of red pepper.

This is one of those recipes I used for Sunday lunch. If you want to have this entree for dinner, you could put the ribs on early in the morning, then at dinner time pour the fat off, add the barbecue sauce and cook until the sauce is hot. I can't always find these ribs; they're the ones that don't look like ribs--

strips of meat about two inches thick and three inches long with a slender bone in each one.

BARBECUED RIBS
1½ to 2 pounds pork ribs
1 recipe barbecue sauce

Put ribs in the crockpot and cook on low overnight. Next morning pour off the fat and broth and add the barbecue sauce; cook several hours more.

BARBECUED CHICKEN
Place chicken pieces in an ovenproof dish. Bake at 350 degrees for thirty minutes. Add barbecue sauce and cook thirty minutes longer.

Most tuna casserole recipes call for mushroom soup and noodles. This one is a change of pace and a quick and easy meal.

TUNA CASSEROLE
1 can (6 ¼ ounce) tuna, drained
¾ cup thinly sliced celery
¼ cup chopped green pepper
¼ teaspoon onion powder
1 can (4 ounce) mushrooms

1 can (10½ ounce) condensed cream of celery soup
1 can French fried onions

Mix first six ingredients and one-half can of onions; place in a greased casserole dish. Bake at 350 degree for 25 minutes. Sprinkle remaining onions on top and bake five minutes longer. Since I don't keep onion powder, I use a small amount of fresh or dehydrated onion.

When I try to fry fish, I can never get it light and flaky, but this baked catfish has the taste of fried without the fat.

BAKED CATFISH
¼ cup yellow cornmeal
¼ cup all purpose flour
¼ cup grated Parmesan cheese
1 teaspoon paprika
½ teaspoon salt
½ teaspoon ground black pepper
Dash of ground red pepper
1 egg white
2 tablespoons skim milk
4 (4 ounce) catfish fillets
Butter flavored cooking spray

Combine cornmeal, flour, cheese, paprika, salt and peppers; set aside. Wisk together egg white and milk. Dip fillets in milk mixture and dredge in cornmeal mixture. Place fillets in a non-stick pan coated with cooking spray. Coat each fillet with cooking spray. Bake at 350 degrees 30 minutes or until fish flakes easily when tested with a fork.

Buttermilk works just as well as the egg white/milk mixture and is much simpler to use. I mix the first seven ingredients directly on waxed paper. Then it is ready to dredge the fish and I don't have an extra bowl to wash.

SALMON CROQUETTES
THE OLD WAY AND DRESSED UP
Salmon croquettes were a mainstay in my diet during my growing up years, probably because canned salmon was an inexpensive, nutritious way to feed a family. No doubt this is another recipe that's not written down anywhere, but most likely one that mothers all over the South prepared at least once a week during the forties and fifties, possibly on into the sixties. Recently I found a recipe for salmon croquettes that are light

and fluffy and taste more like crab cakes than salmon, and a recipe that combines salmon and crabmeat.

SALMON CROQUETTES LIKE MAMA MADE
1 can (15 ounce) salmon
¼ cup flour
1 egg
Oil to fry

Combine salmon, flour, and egg. Make into patties. Fry over moderately high heat until brown on both sides. Mama didn't drain the salmon, so I don't either. I took out the bones until I read that I should leave them in because they are loaded with nutrition.

NEW SALMON CROQUETTES
1 can (15 ½ ounce) salmon
2 green onions, chopped
½ cup dry seasoned breadcrumbs
1 egg
Vegetable oil

Drain salmon; place in a bowl and flake with a fork. Thinly slice green onions and add them to the salmon along with 2 tablespoons breadcrumbs and egg. Mix to blend well. Form 6 patties. Dip the patties in the remaining breadcrumbs to coat. Heat about ¼ inch oil in a large skillet over medium heat. Add salmon patties and cook, turning once, until both sides are crisp and golden and the croquettes are heated through, about 7 minutes total.

SALMON CRABMEAT PATTIES
1 can (6 ounce) salmon
1 can (4 ounce) crabmeat
2 tablespoons bread crumbs
½ teaspoon red pepper
1-2 green onions, chopped
1 egg
Cooking oil

Mix ingredients together. Shape into four to six patties. Fry on each side until golden brown.

HARD TO FIND RECIPES

Macaroni Pie

Potato Salad

Creamed Potatoes

Gravy made with flour

Gravy made with cornstarch

Dumplings

Chili

Baked Beans

We Southern cooks make dishes all the time that are not written down anywhere; at least I haven't found them. We either learned them from our mothers or other relatives, or else through trial and error we came up with our unique recipe. In this section I want to share how I prepare these Southern foods. Once I was in a group of women who were discussing how they make macaroni pie. We couldn't even agree on a name, for example: macaroni and cheese, cheese and macaroni, cheese pie, macaroni pie. Everyone had a different method, which they and their family all loved. Here's the recipe my family likes and how it came to be.

I FINALLY LEARNED TO MAKE
MACARONI PIE

When my older son was about eight, he earnestly asked me one day, "Mama, why can't you make macaroni pie like people take to covered dish dinners and reunions?"

I was taken aback. Hadn't I discovered a marvelous frozen macaroni and cheese dish in a tinfoil pan that, when baked, was a golden yellow, cheesy and bubbling? The rest of the family hadn't complained. But I hadn't fooled this child. The macaroni pie wasn't homemade and it certainly wasn't Southern.

It wasn't that I hadn't tried to make a macaroni pie, but I was never pleased with the results. That's one of those recipes you won't find in any cookbook, even books compiled by schools and churches. You might find one that tells you to make a white sauce, or add onions, or a bread topping, but that isn't Southern Macaroni Pie. I guess we're supposed to be born knowing how to prepare this dish.

Finally, I asked my sister, who could put together a mean macaroni pie, how she did it. "I use two eggs," she replied, as if she were sharing a family secret.

She assumed I knew more than I did. "What else do you use?" I gently prodded.

"A cup of everything," she answered nonchalantly. Now she really was assuming too much.

"You take a cup of macaroni, cook it, and add one cup of cheese and one cup of milk?" I persisted.

"You got it," she said.

Even I could figure it out from there, and the recipe is listed below.

MACARONI PIE
1 cup macaroni
2 eggs
Salt and pepper to taste
1 cup milk
1 cup cheddar cheese, cubed
Butter or margarine

Cook macaroni according to package directions; drain. Beat eggs with salt and pepper; add milk and mix thoroughly. Add cooked macaroni and cubed cheese; dot with butter. Bake, uncovered, at 350 degrees for twenty minutes.

Take dish out of the oven while it still looks a little underdone. Don't overcook, or it will be dry. Stir and cover. It will thicken as it sets. Follow these directions and you, too, can make macaroni pie like people take to reunions and covered dish dinners.

One advantage to this recipe is you can prepare any size that suits your family; it is easy to double, triple, or cut in half. To save dishwashing, grease a casserole dish and beat the eggs directly in the baking dish. Slowly add milk, a little salt and pepper, and continue beating until blended before adding macaroni and cheese.

HEALTH TIPS: I hate to think how much fat and cholesterol this dish contains. But there is hope. You can use low-fat cheese. You can substitute 2%, 1% or skim milk. You can omit the margarine, using Butter Buds instead. You can cut down on the salt. You can use egg whites instead of whole eggs (two whites per egg). When using regular cheese, I use medium sharp because I think mild is too mild and sharp is too sharp. However, now that I use low fat cheese, I use sharp because medium is not sharp enough. You can load this dish with fat and cholesterol or make it as fat and cholesterol free as you desire, but the original recipe is so good!

POTATO SALAD

6-8 medium potatoes, cut in cubes
1 teaspoon salt
1 small onion chopped
1 stalk celery, chopped
2 tablespoons chopped pickle
1 jar (2 ounce) chopped pimento
1/2 cup mayonnaise
1 tablespoon prepared mustard
2 boiled eggs (optional)
Paprika

Peel about six small potatoes and cut into cubes. Add about one teaspoon salt. Add enough water so that you can see it, but don't completely cover potatoes. Cook potatoes until tender, about ten minutes. Pour off water.

Mix all ingredients then mix gently with potatoes. I mix the potato salad in the pot I cooked the potatoes in then put the salad in a dish and sprinkle it with paprika.

If I add boiled eggs, I wash the egg and place in the pot with potatoes while they are cooking. Let cool slightly then grate into salad.

CREAMED POTATOES

Peel about six small potatoes and cut into cubes. Red potatoes work best for creaming. Add about one teaspoon salt. Add enough water so that you can see it, but don't completely cover potatoes. Cook potatoes until tender, about 10 minutes. Pour off water. Add butter to taste, mix in cooking pot with electric mixer. Add milk, beat until creamy.

If you don't want to take time to cream potatoes, pour water off and add either butter or Butter Buds. This makes a tasty side dish with a minimum of fuss.

BASIC GRAVY
(made with flour and fat)
Use grease left when frying meat such as chicken, steak or pork chops. Pour grease out of pan and add back two tablespoons of grease. Stir in two tablespoons of flour, salt and pepper, and cook, stirring constantly, until mix is a golden brown. Slowly stir in one cup milk, broth, or water. Bring to a boil, stirring constantly. Cook until thick and smooth.

Whole milk doesn't require as much thickening as broth or water. You may want to add more flour when using water or broth. Double or triple this recipe as needed.

CORNSTARCH GRAVY
(made with broth and no fat)
Measure two cups broth in pan. Mix three tablespoons cornstarch in cold water. Add to broth. Cook until thick. You may want to use more or less cornstarch, depending on the desired thickness of gravy. Never add cornstarch to hot liquid. If you do, you will have a lumpy mess on your hands. That's why recipes say to use a whisk the entire time the gravy is cooking. If you use cold broth, you don't have to get rid of lumps because there aren't any.

MY SISTERS DIDN'T BELIEVE
I COULD MAKE MAMA'S DUMPLINGS

At a family gathering I made chicken and dumplings. My sisters started having a fit, demanding to know how I could make dumplings just like Mama's when they had failed in all their efforts. I wasn't aware that I was doing anything out of the ordinary; I had made dumplings for my family for years. When pressed for an answer, all I could say was that I used to watch Mama make them—that's the osmosis part of my learning to cook. I've never seen a recipe for this type dumplings, and I've never talked with anyone who makes them like this.

When my older son was little, this was one of his favorite meals. It was not one of my husband's, so he always suggested we have company to help eat the dumplings so he wouldn't see them again. Lately he's come to appreciate them, too. Now we always have dumplings during the Christmas holidays.

One summer while the extended family was at the beach, we prepared a meal at my niece's apartment; she had requested chicken and dumplings. My sister, who thinks she can't make dumplings, had brought noodles which she forgot to take to the apartment. I offered to make real dumplings.

They had all the necessary ingredients and equipment except a rolling pin. Not to be outdone, I used a 64-ounce soft drink bottle. The dumplings were a big hit, especially with my niece's roommate, a Yankee who had never before tasted Southern cooking like this. I'm not sure too many Southerners have, either.

Before I make dumplings, I cook a hen. The hardest part of cooking the hen is getting the chastity belt out of it. That's the crooked piece of metal, impossible to remove, used to fasten the hen's legs together. After working ten minutes getting this unnecessary piece of wire loose, I take out the extra pieces inside the hen. Check the other end because the neck is there. I'm sure Mama found something to do with these pieces, but I discard them.

I place the hen in a big pot, breast side down and add two to three cups of water. Bring the water to a boil and simmer two to three hours. When the hen is tender, take it out of the pot and pour the broth in a container so you can skim off the fat. Pour the almost fat-free broth back in the pot. Usually I leave just a little fat for flavor. Bring the broth to a boil before adding dumplings.

DUMPLINGS
2 cups self-rising flour
8-10 tablespoons shortening (Crisco)
3-4 tablespoons milk

Mix shortening into flour, add milk, and make dough into a ball. Mama used milk instead of water in piecrust because she said, "it does better," and that was reason enough for me.

Roll thin, like piecrust. Cut into narrow strips; drop in boiling chicken broth one strip at a time. Cook, covered, about 15 minutes. Stir gently once or twice during cooking.

Sometimes I make the dough ahead, roll it in waxed paper and place in a plastic bag. When I'm ready to cook, I unroll it and cut into strips.

HAVING HOMEMADE HOT DOGS WAS AN ADVENTURE WHEN I WAS A CHILD

I was a child during World War II and for some unknown reason (maybe it was to conserve energy), hot dog and hamburger buns often were not sliced. Notice I said often. Not every time. And often Mama would absent-mindedly pick up the hot dog buns, thinking they weren't sliced, and slice them again on the other side.

To make matters worse, Mama didn't know she wasn't supposed to boil wieners, so she boiled them five minutes or so until they doubled in size. Imagine six-year-old hands trying to hold a hot dog bun sliced on both sides, filled with a wiener twice the size it should be, topped with chili that kept falling off. Eating Mama's hot dogs became a real challenge.

In spite of her comedy of errors with hot dogs, Mama redeemed herself with her chili. When people ask me for my chili recipe, which I learned from Mama, and I tell them I use only ground beef, chili powder and salt, they look at me as if they think I'm hoarding an old family recipe.

I've thought long and hard about the chili I make, trying to decide what makes it different. I've finally decided the secret of making chili everyone raves about is twofold: my chili is not greasy, and it has an even texture. To make chili, I use about one and one-half pounds ground beef. I think ground chuck has the best flavor, better even than ground round, but you can use ordinary hamburger if you wish.

Place the meat in a boiler and cover with water. Cook over medium high heat, stirring constantly until all the pink is gone. If you are alone in the house and the phone or doorbell rings, don't answer either (unless you have a cordless phone) because lumps can appear in chili in seconds. If one of the children comes running in shouting that the house is on fire, remove the pot from the stove before checking out their report.

After the meat is browned, strain it. Return the strained meat to the pot and again cover with water, but just barely. Add about one teaspoon of salt. Here's the hard part. Add chili powder until the meat turns the right color. I would estimate about one tablespoon of chili powder per pound of meat. Experiment until you get the chili hot or mild enough to suit your family's taste.

I've heard that chili needs to cook for hours, and that depends on the amount of time I have. Often I bring the chili to a boil and simmer only a few minutes before serving. At our house, I put out all the fixings and everyone makes their own hot dogs.

This chili freezes well. Make a double batch and freeze the leftovers. Then when you need to have a meal in a hurry, thaw and warm. If you've had an especially hectic day, you can prop up your feet while the family takes care of themselves.*

CHILI
1½ to 2 pounds ground chuck
1 teaspoon salt (or less)
1 to 2 tablespoons chili powder

Cover ground beef with water; stir constantly until all pink is gone. Drain. Cover meat again with water. Add salt and chili powder, stirring well. Simmer until you're ready to eat.

*You may first have to train your family to take care of themselves. I began working fulltime the summer my boys were twenty-two and fourteen, and both were working with their dad. Since they were accustomed to having a meal on the table when they walked in the door, that summer was quite an adjustment for all of us.

They came in each night like ravenous wolves. I began working in the middle of May, and that whole summer my three males paced the kitchen like caged animals while I tried to prepare supper. I couldn't yell at them to get out of the kitchen and leave me alone, because they talked about their day's events as they paced, and I might miss something I really wanted to hear. They kept me entertained, if anyone needs to be entertained while cooking.

On the days they got home before I did, I found them already pacing. They created an obstacle course, and I had to ease my body toward the stove, dodging them as I went. More exhausted than usual one night, I warmed the chili, heated the wieners and buns, and sat down at the table. I told them they would have to bring everything to the table because I was too tired to move.

All three of them sat down at the table with me. We all looked at each other. Finally one of them noticed we didn't have any plates, and got them. Another saw we needed silverware and napkins. Another caught on that he should bring the chili, buns and wieners to the table. Still we needed mustard, catsup and onions--glasses needed to be filled with ice and tea poured.

I lost count of the number of times these male members of my family got up before they finally got everything we needed on the table so that we could eat our hot dogs.

Would you say that I had spoiled them?

Baked beans are always good with hot dogs. You may recognize this recipe as the barbecue sauce I use on my meat loaf and you'd be right. I've also used it with tomato sauce and canned tomatoes to make spaghetti sauce.

BAKED BEANS
1 can (16 ounce) pork and beans
2 tablespoons brown sugar
2 tablespoons vinegar
1 tablespoon Worcestershire sauce
1 teaspoon dry mustard
Chopped onion

Mix brown sugar, vinegar, Worcestershire sauce and dry mustard together, stir into beans. Add chopped onion if desired. Cook at 350 degrees 30 minutes.

Sometimes when I feel tired or lazy and don't want to chop onion, I used dehydrated onion.

DID YOU BRING EVERYTHING
WE NEED FOR THE HAYRIDE?

Let me warn you up front that this vignette doesn't contain a recipe; instead it is a story about hot dogs.

Marion and I have chaperoned enough youth groups that we consider ourselves pros—almost--and we've found that teenagers never want to go on a hayride unless the temperature is 30 degrees or below. Never in the spring, fall, or summer does a hayride enter their minds, but let the temperature start dropping, and no other type social event will suit them.

Finally one winter we quit fighting. They wanted to go on a hayride to Table Rock State Park in the middle of November, and we said, "Okay." The kids rode in the back of a truck while we saner adults rode in closed vehicles with heaters. Having been to several cookouts at Table Rock in the dead of winter, Marion and I knew what to expect. On this particular weekend, the weatherman was predicting temperatures in the low twenties, and this time he was right on target.

Undaunted, we neither postponed nor cancelled the trip. Instead, we fortified ourselves. I borrowed my older son's thermal underwear and his wool socks. Then I put on jeans, a warm shirt and a 100 percent wool sweater I can't normally wear unless there's snow on the ground. I took a heavy jacket, my toboggan cap and gloves. Marion was dressed similarly in his outdoor gear.

The three of us (our younger son was a teenager) scurried around the house, trying to get ready. Now the temperature had not yet fallen in the low twenties, and we were operating out of a warm house. After we got all that protective clothing on, we had to move fast, so we all got in the car and drove to the church where we met our group.

As we drove toward Table Rock, we discussed other youth trips we had been on and how remiss some of the chaperones had been. We were congratulating ourselves for remembering to bring everything we could possibly need to take to a shelter in the wilderness—a flashlight, light bulbs, a drop cord, a socket for the drop cord in case there was no place to plug the coffee pot, fuses, trash bags--even matches--all those items crucial for comfort that you usually forget.

Then we made the turn at the sign that reads: Table Rock State Park. That's when I remembered. I had forgotten the food—the chili I had made earlier, the wieners, the mustard, catsup, pickles--everything perishable was back home, twenty miles away, in my refrigerator.

What could we do? If you've ever been on this type outing, you know they're unorganized at best. While everyone else was unloading, building a fire, making hot chocolate in the coffee pot, huddling together trying to stay warm, Marion and I slipped away to the nearest phone, called our son at home and asked him to bring the food to us.

That meant the delay of a twenty-mile drive instead of forty miles if we had to go back home ourselves. We eased back in with the crowd and helped the other chaperones finish setting up. Our son made great time so we were able to eat our hot dogs without having to wait too long. In fact, I don't think most of the kids ever realized what a dumb thing we had done. We certainly didn't announce it.

Or maybe they were too numb with cold to comprehend what was happening, because most of them, despite our re-peated warnings, were dressed as if they were going to a foot-ball game on a warm evening.

After that fateful outing, every time thereafter, before we left the driveway someone would always ask, "Do we have the food?" And never again did we feel quite as smug about our ability to remember everything we needed for a cookout.

CASSEROLES

Squash Casserole

Broccoli Casserole

Sweet Potato Soufflé

Until I started compiling this cookbook, I didn't realize how few casseroles I make, but these three are too good to leave out. Since they don't fit anywhere else, I'm including them in this short section on casseroles.

The broccoli casserole as well as the squash casserole are good to take to covered dish meals, or to make for Thanksgiving, Christmas, or other times when the family is together, because each of them serves 8 to 10. If the stuffing mix starts to get too brown on either of these casseroles, cover the dish with a lid or tinfoil for the remaining cooking time. The broccoli casserole freezes well, but the squash casserole doesn't because of the sour cream.

SQUASH CASSEROLE
1 can (10 ½ ounce) cream of chicken soup
1 container (8 ounce) sour cream
1 onion, grated
2 raw carrots, grated
2 pounds squash, cooked

TOPPING
1 package (10 ounce) Pepperidge Farm stuffing mix
1 stick butter or margarine

Combine soup, sour cream, grated onion and grated carrots. Fold in cooked squash and place in dish. Melt butter, toss stuffing lightly. Spread on top of casserole. Bake at 325 degrees 40 to 45 minutes. One-half package stuffing and ½ stick butter works just as well if you don't want all that topping.

UNUSUAL BROCCOLI CASSEROLE EASES TENSION AT BRIDESMAIDS' LUNCHEON
According to the wedding etiquette book, if none of the bridesmaids offer to give the bridesmaids' luncheon, the duty falls on the bride's family. Since all of my daughter's bridesmaids lived out-of-town, and it was not convenient for them to

give the luncheon, and we were following the etiquette book to the letter, my sisters and I hosted the bridesmaids' luncheon on the day of the wedding.

Several obstacles stood in the way, not the least of which was the stress and strain of the wedding itself, since the bridesmaids' luncheon traditionally is held on the day of the wedding. Because I didn't have a dining room, and I could not seat the number we wanted to invite anywhere except on my patio, I considered an outdoor luncheon. But the bride and her father were too paranoid about the possibility of rain to even entertain this thought.

When I realized they were not even going to consider an outdoor luncheon, I asked a close friend who does have a dining room, and an adjacent living room where tables could be set up for the overflow, to let me use her house for a couple of hours the day of the wedding. I assured her I would bring the food, do all the preparation and clean up afterward. All she had to do was to look pretty and smile. She didn't give me an immediate answer and without consulting me, asked another friend for the use of her house.

The second friend graciously consented, though we were not close enough for me to make such a request, and I would never have done it on my own. This immediately put a strain on all of us. To further complicate matters, the groom's family are more prim and proper than we, and my daughter was concerned that we do everything right since all of the female members of the groom's family from out of town would be attending.

With the help of my two sisters, Bette and Louise, we planned a menu we were comfortable with--good Southern food. My mother-in-law offered to cook her delicious creamed corn. Bette agreed to make the broccoli casserole. Though I had made this casserole many times, it was a new recipe for Bette, and she is famous for adding to or taking away from recipes— not necessarily to make them better—she just follows her whims. I cautioned her to make the dish once for her family as a trial run. She assured me that she would.

As it turned out, we had the bridesmaids' luncheon outside anyway; I don't know what the bride and her father thought about that—I didn't ask them. We set up a buffet table in the breakfast room, and everyone was to sit around the swimming pool to eat. The hostess had rented several umbrella tables. The day dawned bright and clear and not too hot--perfect weather for an outdoor luncheon (which could have been held on my patio). About thirty guests assembled at noon, excited about the wedding which was scheduled for seven o'clock. Everything was going just as planned--flawless.

Playing the perfect hostesses, Bette, Louise and I stood around making conversation, watching to see that everyone had what they needed, and waited until last to serve ourselves. We did notice that no one was getting any broccoli casserole--even the bride passed it up--and it was one of her favorite dishes.

After everyone had gone through the line, I started serving my plate; Bette and Louise were behind me. When I tried to dip the spoon into the broccoli casserole, I hit resistance. It felt like a celery stalk covered with soup. I turned to Bette and asked, "Did you cook this broccoli?"

"Was I supposed to cook it?" she asked, startled.

I started laughing. All the tension I had felt during the weeks and months of planning my only daughter's wedding was released. I couldn't stop laughing. Bette and Louise joined me. We were making such a scene that we had to retreat into the kitchen so our guests couldn't hear us. Finally we composed ourselves enough to serve our plates and join the rest of the party.

The recipe calls for frozen chopped broccoli. You are supposed to cook the broccoli, drain it, and then add the other ingredients. Bette had bought whole frozen broccoli--I don't think she even thawed it--put it in the casserole dish and covered it with the other ingredients. In forty minutes cooking time, the broccoli barely got warm and didn't even begin to get tender.

We wonder what all those ladies thought when they tried to serve their plates and couldn't make a dent in the broccoli casserole. This incident was a tension reliever that helped me get through the wedding. We didn't tell the bride for a long, long time about the uncooked broccoli casserole.

Another thing we didn't tell her for a long time was that we borrowed one of her wedding gifts—a dinner plate. It was the same pattern as the hostess's and she was one plate short. After the luncheon we returned the plate to her display no worse for the use.

BROCCOLI CASSEROLE
1 egg
½ cup mayonnaise
1 can (10 ½ ounce) cream of mushroom soup
1 medium onion, chopped
2 packages (10 ounce) chopped broccoli,
cooked and drained
½ to 1 cup grated cheddar cheese

TOPPING
½ package Pepperidge Farm Herb Stuffing
½ stick butter or margarine

Beat egg slightly; add mayonnaise, mushroom soup, and chopped onion. Blend in cooked broccoli. (Cook broccoli about 5 minutes after it comes to a boil). Pour into a two-quart casserole dish. Cover with grated cheese. Melt ½ stick butter or margarine, mix with herb stuffing. Pour over broccoli mixture. Bake at 325 degrees for 40 to 45 minutes.

I tried many ways to make sweet potato soufflé before I found this recipe. After I cooked it once, I disregarded all the others. This one is the best. I also tried variations of the cereal-nut-flour-butter topping. I forgot them, too. Though those toppings are delicious, they don't go well with this recipe, I think because of the pineapple and sherry.

SWEET POTATO SOUFFLE
4 pounds sweet potatoes
½ cup butter
¼ cup firmly packed brown sugar
½ teaspoon salt
½ cup honey
¼ cup sherry
1 can (8 ounce) crushed pineapple
½ bag (10 ounce) marshmallows

Cook whole potatoes until tender, peel. Add butter. (Hot potatoes will melt the butter.) Add brown sugar, salt and honey. Mix well with a mixer or food processor. The processor will produce a creamier mixture. Stir in sherry and pineapple. Bake in greased 1½-quart casserole at 350 degrees 30 to 40 minutes. I cook the casserole for 30 minutes or so and add the marshmallows, then cook another five or six minutes. The marshmallows will get too brown if you cook them the entire time.

BREADS

Angel Biscuits

Whipped Cream Biscuits

Easy Rolls

Cornbread

Cornbread Mix

Sourdough Bread

Fat-free Brown Bread

HOMEMADE VERSUS STORE BOUGHT

When I was growing up, I thought if store-bought or restaurant food was good, then homemade was even better. With that misconception in mind, I tried for years to make coffeecakes and cinnamon rolls that would melt in my family's mouth. Most of my efforts not only didn't melt in their mouths, they weren't even edible. Now, when I want a really good coffeecake, cinnamon rolls, or Danish pastry, I go to the bakery. I finally gave up on anything containing yeast, except for angel biscuits.

* * *

An angel biscuit, aptly named, is light, fluffy and delightful. Making angel biscuits is always an adventure for me because mine never turn out the same way twice, but however I make them, they're always delicious. I think my biggest problem is that I have several recipes, each one with its own unique directions.

At least they all agree on ingredients. Or do they? A friend told me she uses self-rising flour. Listed below are both recipes; one with plain flour and the other with self-rising. The self-rising recipe works just as well, and if you choose this route, you don't have to add baking powder, soda and salt.

ANGEL BISCUITS
(with plain flour)
1 package active dry yeast
2 tablespoons warm water
5 cups plain flour
¼ cup sugar
1 tablespoon baking powder
1 teaspoon soda
1 teaspoon salt
1 cup shortening (Crisco)
2 cups buttermilk (at room temperature)

ANGEL BISCUITS
(with self-rising flour)
1 package active dry yeast
2 tablespoons warm water
5 cups self-rising flour
¼ cup sugar
1 cup shortening (Crisco)
2 cups buttermilk (at room temperature)

Dissolve yeast in warm water. Add dissolved yeast to buttermilk, mixing well. Sift dry ingredients. Cut shortening into dry ingredients. Add buttermilk, mixing just enough to blend. Choose a method below, then bake the biscuits at 425 degrees for 10 minutes.

After mixing the dough, you can go in several directions. One recipe says to place dough in greased bowl. Let stand five minutes. Pat with hand covered in oil. Place in refrigerator for at least three hours. When you are ready to bake the biscuits, use just enough flour to roll out and cut.

Another recipe say to mix ingredients, cover bowl and place in refrigerator overnight. Pinch off dough in biscuit-sized pieces, place pieces of dough on ungreased pan, handling as little as possible.

Still another recipe instructs us to place dough on a floured cloth and knead about one minute. Roll out; cut with cutter, place on ungreased cookie sheet and bake--no instructions about refrigeration or rising.

A recipe which came off a flour sack says to knead the dough 25 to 30 times before placing it in a lightly greased bowl. Cover and refrigerate at least three hours but no longer than three days.

Evelyn Nalley McCollum

A friend says she never refrigerates the dough because she can never get the biscuits mixed up ahead of time. She lets the dough rise in the bowl then bakes the bread immediately. When I tried her method, I let the biscuits rise a second time after I cut them. These biscuits rose beautifully and were akin to rolls.

Choose a method that appeals to you, or try all of them and see which works for you. I'm sure that how much time you have to prepare will be a factor in which method you choose.

I recently heard that a cousin always used two packages of yeast. I tried that and was very pleased with the results. Also, I have a tendency to roll my dough too thin—experiment to see the size biscuits you want. I think it works best to let the buttermilk come to room temperature before mixing. And shortening now comes in those marvelous one-cup portions, which makes measuring so much easier.

ANYONE CAN MAKE THESE BISCUITS
This is the most simple biscuit recipe I have ever found. You may wonder why it doesn't call for shortening, but when you think how much fat eight ounces of whipping cream contains, you know the answer. A cousin gave me this recipe and she said to bake them on a flat iron frying pan. If you have one, use it, but I don't think the type pan is crucial to the success of these biscuits.

WHIPPED CREAM BISCUITS
2 cups self-rising flour
1 carton (eight ounce) whipping cream

Mix flour with whipping cream. Roll out dough, cut biscuits, place on ungreased cookie sheet, bake at 450 degrees for 10 minutes.

EASY ROLLS
2 cups self-rising flour
1 teaspoon sugar
1/3 cup mayonnaise (not low-fat or fat-free)
1 cup milk

Mix all four ingredients and drop dollops of dough into a greased muffin tin. Bake about 10 minutes at 450 degrees. Skim milk will work with these rolls; the more fat content in the milk the richer the rolls will be.

DID YOU GET YOUR CORNBREAD OUT OF THE LARD BUCKET?
One night Great Aunt Lillie was having supper with us, and she was taking on about how good my cornbread was. "Did you get it out of the lard bucket?" she asked, smacking her lips.

I asked her to repeat her question. Aunt Lillie naturally talked in a loud voice, but in answer to my question she asked again, "Did you get it out of the lard bucket?" This time she raised her voice slightly.

I heard each word clearly, but since I didn't understand her question, again I asked, like a dummy, "What did you say?"

By now she thought my hearing was impaired, and she fairly shouted across the table, enunciating every word, "I-said-did-you-get-your-cornbread-out-of-the-lard-bucket?"

Her shout brought Mama out of whatever reverie she was in, and coming to my defense, she explained, "Aunt Lillie wants to know if you put shortening in your cornbread."

"Of course," I replied, "wasn't I supposed to?" *How else would you make cornbread?* I wondered.

I didn't tell Aunt Lillie, but she would have been surprised to know how long it had taken me to learn to make cornbread anyone could even eat, much less compliment me on. But I kept trying. Early in our marriage I made cornbread and my husband asked me what it was. I had made a small amount and cooked it in a large pan so it would be thin and crispy the way he liked it. For some reason it didn't brown, and it looked like a huge cornmeal pancake.

Mama was an excellent cook, and I often sat with pad in hand, pen poised, picking her brain, but she could never tell me exactly how she made anything because she used a handful of this, a pinch of that and a dab of something else.

Since I was on my own, I tried using recipes in cookbooks or on packages of cornmeal. I knew I didn't want to put sugar in my cornbread, but I was not experienced enough as a cook to know what else to add or eliminate to make the cornbread I envisioned.

After much discussion with Mama and even more experimenting, I came up with almost perfect cornbread. At last I was on the right track, but still my cornbread didn't taste quite like Mama's. I kept asking her what I was doing wrong, and she kept telling me my buttermilk was too sour. (To this day I have not encountered buttermilk that was too sour.)

Finally, one day out of the blue, she said that she added a pinch of soda. "Even if you use self-rising cornmeal and flour?" I asked.

"Yes, if I use buttermilk, I add a pinch of soda," she replied. At last, I had Mama's recipe for cornbread.

Another secret, which I already knew because I had watched her do it often enough, is to put oil in the iron frying pan and put the pan in the oven while the oven preheats. This makes the bread crusty and brown all over.

An even better way to cook cornbread is in a cornstick pan, or in a round pan with partitions. Then it is crusty on all sides.

I must confess that through the years I have discovered that I don't have to put as much lard (shortening, oil) in my cornbread as I did when Aunt Lillie ate with us, and now I use only one tablespoon of oil to one cup of cornbread mix. The cornbread is just as good and much more nutritious.

I've also found that stoneground cornmeal makes better cornbread. It seems the coarser the corn is ground the better the cornbread.

CORNBREAD
1 tablespoon oil
¾ cup self-rising cornmeal
¼ cup self-rising flour
A pinch of soda
1 egg
2/3 cup buttermilk

Drizzle one tablespoon oil in an 8-inch iron frying pan or cornstick pan. Put pan in oven while oven preheats to 450 degrees. Mix cornmeal, flour and soda. Add enough buttermilk to dampen cornmeal and flour, mix in egg, and add remaining buttermilk. Pour mixture in hot pan; cook at 450 degrees 20 minutes. This time and temperature is perfect in my oven but you may have to experiment with yours as oven temperatures vary.

HEALTH TIP: You can substitute two egg whites for one whole egg, but your cornbread won't be quite as high and soft. Also, I use nonfat buttermilk.

Since I make so much cornbread, and since I have become more of a health nut, I make up my cornbread mix ahead of time, and I substitute soy flour for part of the white flour.

CORNBREAD MIX
1½ cups self-rising cornmeal
¼ cup self-rising flour
¼ cup soy flour
1/8 teaspoon soda

I keep mixing this ratio of self-rising cornmeal, self-rising flour, soy flour and soda until I get my Tupperware canister full. When it's time to make cornbread, I take ¾ cup of the mix, one egg, 2/3 cup of buttermilk and mix according to directions above. I bake cornbread in a cornstick pan. If you are using a larger pan, you may need to increase the mix and buttermilk accordingly. I like my batter fairly thick.

I'VE GIVEN UP ON MAKING YEAST BREAD

How I wish I could make yeast bread. I can't even <u>bake</u> yeast bread. Early one morning a friend sent me a fresh loaf of bread ready for the oven. I baked the bread according to her directions and took a mess--pure and simple—out of the oven. The bread was a lovely, golden brown on top and still doughy inside.

My family, who had smelled the unmistakable aroma of fresh bread baking, was terribly upset with me when I served them that half-baked mess, trying to convince them that it was good.

I asked my friend the next time she wanted to give us bread, for my family's sake, to please bake it for me.

"Do you want it sliced and buttered, too?" she asked.

"Just baked will do," I answered.

Soon she brought us another loaf wrapped in a towel in a basket, all baked and sliced, still warm from the oven. We devoured it. Not a crumb was left.

My younger son looked wistfully at me and asked, "Mom, why can't you make bread like this?"

Why not, indeed? The mere words "mix with warm water" and "let rise in a warm place" defeat me. How warm is warm? Where is a warm place?

I had tried to make bread. It was one of those cold, wintry days when I was a fulltime homemaker. I decided there could be no better way to spend a dreary day than by making a loaf of bread.

I took my most trusted cookbook and found a recipe that looked simple enough. I worked on that bread all day long-- mixing it, letting it rise (praying it would rise), punching it down, kneading it, shaping it and placing it in a loaf pan. I had picked a recipe that could be done in one day's time so I could surprise my family that night.

I surprised them all right. The bread had the crustiest top you could imagine. So crusty we needed a chisel and hammer to break through. Immediately under the crust was a cavern from front to back. Under that deep hole lay the worst textured bread you could imagine. If holes make the flavor in bread, that loaf should have been listed in the *Guinness Book of World Records.*

Not wanting to hurt my feelings, my family made a half-hearted attempt to eat the bread and praise my efforts. I fed the leftovers to the birds. I didn't watch to see if they ate it; I didn't want to know.

However, I redeemed myself with my family when I started making sourdough bread. A few years ago, making sourdough bread was a craze in our area, and I got right in the middle of it. The biggest problem with this bread was that after a certain number of hours I was supposed to either feed it, knead it or bake it. If I didn't time it just right, I would find myself up in the middle of the night taking care of this dough, or bread, depending on the stage it was in. It reminded me of caring for a colicky baby.

I was working fulltime then, and often I would take a loaf of freshly baked bread back to work after lunch, because the time had come to bake the bread while I was on my lunch hour.

If you intend to make sourdough bread, I suggest that you read through the directions very carefully, making sure you fully understand before you embark on this bread-making journey.

Before you can even make the bread, you have to make the starter. Below is the recipe which includes the starter. Once the women in a community start making this bread, they share the starter with their friends and neighbors, but it has to begin somewhere.

SOURDOUGH BREAD STARTER
1 package yeast
1 cup warm water
3 tablespoons instant potatoes
¾ cup sugar

Dissolve yeast in small amount of warm water. Add the rest of the water, instant potatoes and sugar, stir until well blended. **Let set on counter eight hours, then keep in refrigerator from three to five days.**

Mix the following three ingredients and add to starter.
1 cup warm water
¾ cup sugar
3 tablespoons instant potatoes

Keep starter out of refrigerator eight to twelve hours. Mixture will be bubbly. Now you're finally ready to make your sourdough bread.

SOURDOUGH BREAD
1 cup starter
½ cup corn oil
1½ cups warm water
1/3 cup sugar
6 cups bread flour
1 tablespoon salt

In a large mixing bowl, make a stiff batter of the ingredients listed above. Place in a well-greased bowl, turning to grease top. Cover greased top lightly with towel and let stand overnight (do not refrigerate).

Next morning punch dough down. Knead a little, divide into three parts. Knead each piece separately. Put into three greased loaf pans and brush with oil. Cover with waxed paper.

Let stand four to five hours. Bake at 350 degrees for 30 to 45 minutes. Remove from pan and brush with butter. Cool on rack. Wrap well to store. Refrigerate or freeze.

TIP: Bread flour can get old. If your bread fails to rise, the problem could be your bread flour. Also, check the date on the yeast package when making the starter.

If you're trying to stay away from fat in all forms and cutting down on sugar, the following is a good recipe for a snack. In the past peanut butter and crackers were a staple, but now almost all crackers contain transfats, the latest buzz word for food we are trying to avoid.

Unless you're extremely nutrition conscious, you'll probably feel about this recipe like you do about my oatmeal. However, it contains whole wheat flour, buttermilk, molasses and raisins—all good for you—and doesn't contain fat, eggs and sugar—not good for you.

Since no one in the family except me will touch this bread, after baking and cooling, I cut the entire loaf into fairly thin slices. I put peanut butter between two slices, then cut that in half. I freeze these mini-sandwiches. When I need a nutritious snack with my hot tea, coffee, or hot chocolate, I take a piece or two out of the freezer and microwave it for a few seconds. I'll have to admit it's not as crunchy and good as crackers, but I keep telling myself how nutritious it is.

FAT-FREE BROWN BREAD
2 cups whole wheat flour
1 cup white flour
2 teaspoons soda
½ teaspoon salt
2 cups buttermilk
½ cup molasses
1 cup raisins

Sift together dry ingredients. Stir in milk and molasses. Add raisins. Let batter stand in loaf pan one hour. Cook at 325 degrees for one hour.

BREAKFAST FOODS

Sausage Breakfast Casserole

Cheesy Grits Casserole

Hot Fruit Bake

Crescent Coffee Cake

Buttermilk Oatmeal Pancakes

Buckwheat Pancakes

Oatmeal

Oatmeal Mix

GOURMET BREAKFAST HAS BECOME
CHRISTMAS TRADITION

I discovered my gourmet breakfast recipes—Sausage Breakfast Casserole, Cheesy Grits, Hot Fruit Bake, and Crescent Coffee Cake--while my children were still home, and this breakfast quickly became a tradition for our family on Christmas morning. Like all families with married children, we sometimes have trouble scheduling our time together during the holiday season, but we try very hard to have all the family here for our gourmet breakfast, though it is not always on Christmas morning.

Before I gained the stamina I now have as the result of a proper diet and regular exercise, often I was exhausted from all the activities and dreaded starting on these casseroles. I had to drag myself into the kitchen and force myself to start to work. Now that our children are grown, often the entire family gathers in the kitchen the night before and we all work together preparing this meal.

These recipes are also wonderful for entertaining either at breakfast or a brunch. Mix them up the night before and slide them in the oven the next morning. Take advantage of the hour they are cooking to take care of last minute details before your guests arrive.

SAUSAGE BREAKFAST CASSEROLE
6 slices bread
Butter or margarine
1 pound bulk sausage
6 ounce shredded cheddar cheese
6 eggs
2 cups half and half
1 teaspoon salt

Remove crusts from bread; spread slices with butter on both sides. (Sometimes I use the new crustless bread.) Butter the sides of a 13 x 9 x 2 baking dish. Place bread in baking dish and set aside. Cook sausage until browned, stirring to crumble; drain well. Spoon sausage over bread slices.

Add salt to eggs, slowly add half-and-half and beat until well mixed. Pour mixture over bread-sausage-mixture. Sprinkle grated cheese on top. Cover casserole and chill overnight. Remove from refrigerator 15 minutes before baking. Bake casserole, uncovered, at 350 degrees for 45 minutes or until set.

Since I have become health conscious, sometimes I use low fat cheese and fat free half-and-half in the sausage casserole. Other times I make it with all the good, fattening ingredients— telling myself it's okay once a year. It depends on how I feel at the time. These lower fat ingredients work just as well. The only difference is that the dish is not quite as rich.

I usually make plain grits because the other dishes have so much butter, eggs and cheese in them, but this is a good recipe to use if you want to dress up grits on occasion.

CHEESY GRITS CASSEROLE
1½ cups regular grits (not instant or quick cooking)
½ cup butter or margarine
12 ounces shredded medium-sharp Cheddar cheese
1 tablespoon Worcestershire sauce
2 teaspoons paprika, divided
3 eggs, beaten

Cook grits according to package directions. Add butter and cheese; stir until melted. Add Worcestershire sauce and one teaspoon paprika, mixing well. Add a small amount of hot grits to eggs, stirring well; stir egg mixture into remaining grits. Pour grits into a lightly greased 2-quart baking dish; sprinkle with remaining teaspoon paprika. Cover and refrigerate overnight. Remove from refrigerator 15 minutes before baking. Bake, uncovered, at 325 degrees for one hour.

HOT FRUIT BAKE
1 can (20 ounce) pineapple tidbits
1 can (17 ounce) apricot halves
1 can (16 ounce) peach halves
1 can (16 ounce) pear halves
1 jar (15 ounce) apple rings
½ cup butter or margarine
½ cup sugar
2 tablespoons cornstarch
1 cup dry sherry

Drain fruit, cut in bite-sized pieces, put in 2-quart casserole and set aside. Melt butter in a small saucepan. Combine sugar and cornstarch; stir into butter. Gradually stir in sherry; cook over low heat, stirring constantly, until thickened and smooth. Pour mixture over fruit; cover and refrigerate overnight. Remove from refrigerator 15 minutes before baking. Bake, uncovered, at 350 degrees for 30 minutes.

I wait until the next morning to make this coffeecake; I'm afraid it would get soggy if I let it sit overnight.

CRESCENT COFFEE CAKE
¾ cup preserves (any fruit of your choice)
2 cans crescent rolls

Separate crescent rolls into triangles. Place a heaping table-spoon of preserves on the wide end of each triangle; roll up starting at the wide end. Place rolls, seam side down, in two rows in a lightly greased 9-inch square pan. Bake at 375 degrees for 30 minutes or until golden brown. Serve warm.

To make these rolls more festive, try these suggestions: spread the rolls with one-fourth cup butter or margarine before adding fruit; add coconut to the preserves; sprinkle baked rolls with powdered sugar after baking.

PANCAKES, BOTH DELICIOUS AND FILLING

Making pancakes for Sunday breakfast became a tradition when my older son was a preschooler. He was an early riser, and he and I would go in the kitchen and make pancakes while his daddy and sister slept a few more minutes. He loved to sit on the cabinet and watch the shortening melt in the electric fry pan while I mixed the batter. My children still consider pan-cakes a treat and I make them every time we're together for breakfast.

I've often heard several people say that they loved pan-cakes but were starved a couple of hours later because the pan-cakes didn't stay with them. I've found this marvelous recipe for hearty pancakes made from several grains that are very fill-ing.

Not only do these pancakes, with sausage patties, make a good breakfast for company, they also make a quick supper on a cold winter's night when you need a fast meal, or simply are not in the mood for cooking. Add butter, maple syrup, and a fresh cup of coffee, and you couldn't ask for anything better.

I'm giving you several versions of this recipe and explain why I changed it. I have probably adapted this recipe as much as any I've ever used, but in my opinion, it cries out to be changed. To me, that's what cooking is all about. Finding a recipe and adapting it to suit your particular family.

The first time I made these pancakes I reduced the brown sugar and the cinnamon to half because I thought the pancakes would be too sweet and have too much of a cinnamon flavor. I was pleased with the results and have never used the full amount of either. However, the sweet, cinnamon taste may appeal to your family, so you might try them that way the first time. I think with the cinnamon and brown sugar they would taste more like a dessert than a breakfast food.

BUTTERMILK OATMEAL PANCAKES
¾ cup rolled oats (oatmeal)
2½ cups non-fat buttermilk
1 cup all purpose white flour
½ cup whole wheat flour
2 teaspoons baking powder
1 teaspoon baking soda
½ teaspoon salt
1 teaspoon ground cinnamon
¼ cup toasted wheat germ
¼ cup packed light brown sugar
1 large egg
2 large egg whites
2 teaspoons vegetable oil, preferably canola

Combine rolled oats and buttermilk in a small bowl; let rest 20 to 30 minutes to soften oats. In a medium sized bowl, stir together flours, baking powder, baking soda, and salt; stir in cinnamon, wheat germ and brown sugar. In another bowl mix together egg, egg white and one teaspoon oil with whisk or fork. Add the oat mixture and the flour mixture and stir until combined. Heat a nonstick skillet over medium heat and brush lightly with a little of the remaining one-teaspoon oil. Pour batter into skillet; turn after two or three minutes. I recommend either an electric fry pan or a griddle to cook pancakes so that you can control the heat.

To give these pancakes more protein, I often use one-half cup soy flour. Instead of one cup white flour, I use one-half cup soy flour and one-half cup white flour. No one can tell the difference and this makes the pancakes more nutritious. The reason for the egg whites is to reduce cholesterol. Often I use two eggs instead of the egg whites.

To make blueberry pancakes, add one cup fresh blueberries to two cups batter. On occasion I've added one medium Granny Smith apple, chopped, to two cups of batter and received raves from my family. I use one-half teaspoon cinnamon and one-half teaspoon cloves when I use apples.

I have used buckwheat flour in place of the oatmeal and it works well. One advantage in using buckwheat is that you don't have to wait for the rolled oats to soften. When I use buckwheat flour, I mix the dry ingredients ahead of time and store the mixture in the freezer. Usually I double or triple the recipe, and I have a mix, ready to add eggs, milk, and oil. Listed below is the recipe using buckwheat flour instead of oatmeal, substituting soy flour, and reducing the amount of cinnamon and brown sugar.

BUCKWHEAT PANCAKES
¾ cup buckwheat flour
½ cup all purpose white flour
½ cup soy flour
½ cup whole wheat flour
¼ cup toasted wheat germ
2 tablespoons packed light brown sugar
2 teaspoons baking powder
1 teaspoon baking soda
1 teaspoon ground cinnamon (or less)
½ teaspoon salt
1 large egg and 2 large egg whites
2 ½ cups nonfat buttermilk
2 teaspoons vegetable oil, preferably canola

IF YOU'RE NOT A HEALTH NUT,
YOU MAY WANT TO TURN THE PAGE

I didn't like oatmeal as a child. Mama cooked it in water, then added sugar, milk and butter, which took away any health food status that it might claim. I don't like the consistency of oatmeal cooked in water—it's slimy--and milk cools it too much.

However, when all the hoopla started about oat bran, I decided to experiment. In the beginning I used oatmeal and oat bran cooked in skim milk, then added Butter Buds, wheat germ, raisins and honey. Later as I read about how nutritious apricots, flaxseeds and sunflower seeds are, I began to add them to our oatmeal. At first my husband had to force down the oatmeal, but now he actually enjoys it, and we have oatmeal for breakfast almost every morning during the winter months. The recipe below is for one serving, cooked in the microwave.

OATMEAL
¾ cup skim milk
2 tablespoons quick cooking oatmeal
2 tablespoons oat bran
Sprinkle of Butter Bud
1 tablespoon raisins
1 chopped dried apricot
1 tablespoon honey
2 teaspoons wheat germ
2 teaspoons ground flaxseeds
1 tablespoon sunflower seeds

Pour milk into a microwaveable bowl. Add oatmeal and oat bran. Microwave on high 2 minutes; remove from microwave and stir. Sprinkle with Butter Buds, add one apricot, raisins, wheat germ, ground flaxseeds and sunflower seeds. I add one tablespoon honey to Marion's oatmeal but I think the raisins make the oatmeal sweet enough.

You may want to substitute 1% or 2% milk and butter or margarine instead of Butter Buds. We usually buy natural honey in a quart jar and pour it into a smaller squeeze bottle which eliminates the mess of trying to add it with a spoon. If I use wheat germ that is not toasted, I add it to the oatmeal, oat bran mixture before I put it in the microwave. I use a coffee measure, which is 2 tablespoons, to measure oatmeal and oat bran. Talk about nutrition in a bowl—this is it!

You can make your life easier by making a mix. One morning when I was preparing our oatmeal, I looked at the array of ingredients spread out before me. I thought: there has to be a better way. And there is. I came up with this recipe for a mix.

OATMEAL MIX
2 cups old fashioned oatmeal
2 cups oat bran
½ cup wheat germ
½ cup flax seed

Mix ingredients together and store in refrigerator or freezer. To make one cup of oatmeal, add ¼ cup mixture to ¾ cup skim milk and microwave for two minutes. Add Butter Buds, stir, then add raisins, apricots, sunflower seeds and honey if desired.

CAKES

Red Velvet Cake

Carrot Cake

Italian Cream Cake

Chocolate Sheet Cake

Apple Dump Cake

Pound Cake

Butter Pound Cake

Chocolate Pound Cake

Cold Oven Pound Cake

Easy Coconut Cake

One Bowl Cake

Yellow Layer Cake

One Egg Cake

Two Egg Chiffon Cake

Caramel Icing

BUT MAMA, I DON'T *WANT*
A CAKE FROM THE BAKERY

Our youngest child was born on July 3. Since his birthday comes so close to the big July 4th holiday, observing it has always been somewhat of a problem because we usually are going to, coming from, or at the beach on his birthday. If his birthday falls on "going to" day, I bake the cake at home and take it with me. If it falls on "at the beach" day someone bakes his cake while we're there.

The problem arises when his birthday falls on "coming from" day. One year when this happened I stopped by a bakery and picked up his favorite cake, Red Velvet, complete with decorations. I've never seen such an indignant child. He couldn't believe I had bought him a cake.

It's amazing how different the thinking of children and mothers can be. I had always baked birthday cakes for my children and felt a little guilty that I never bought them a fancy one from the bakery. Then I learned that he was insulted with a bakery cake. "It doesn't matter if you don't get the cake baked on my birthday," he said, "just so you bake it."

That year we celebrated his birthday a day late with a homemade Red Velvet cake. The bakery cake went in the freezer and finally ended up at a covered dish dinner where it was appreciated.

I've tried two different icings on this cake. There is the original icing recipe that my son prefers, but since I can never get the lumps out of this icing, I prefer cream cheese, and that's the icing I use when it's not his birthday. But if the cake is especially for him, he gets "lumpy" icing. It's a good idea to start this icing as soon as you put the cake in the oven; otherwise, you'll be all day making this cake.

RED VELVET CAKE
½ cup Crisco
1½ cups sugar
2 eggs
1 teaspoon vanilla
2 tablespoons cocoa
2 ounces red food coloring
2¼ cups plain flour
1 teaspoon salt
1 cup buttermilk
1 teaspoon soda
1 tablespoon vinegar

Cream Crisco and sugar. Add eggs and vanilla. Mix cocoa and red food coloring to make a paste. Add paste to shortening/sugar/egg mixture. Sift flour and salt. Add flour alternately with buttermilk. Mix soda and vinegar, fold into batter. Bake in 2 nine inch or 3 eight inch cake pans at 350 degrees for 25 to 30 minutes.

Sometimes I'm just not in the mood to mix cocoa and red food coloring so I mix the cocoa with the dry ingredients and add the food coloring with the buttermilk. I can't see that it makes any difference. Often I buy only one bottle of food coloring and add a bottle of water to make up for the liquid. I have been known to make a red velvet cake without the food coloring at all. It tastes as good—it just isn't red. It may even taste better. Eating a red cake that tastes chocolate is always a little weird anyway, like eating white chocolate.

ICING FOR RED VELVET CAKE
5 tablespoons plain flour
1 cup whole milk (not skim, 1% or 2%)
1 cup sugar
¼ teaspoon salt
2 sticks butter or margarine
1 teaspoon vanilla

Cook flour and milk until thick, stirring constantly. Let cool. In a mixing bowl, cream sugar, salt and butter, add vanilla. Combine mixtures and spread on cooled cake.

ALTERNATE ICING FOR RED VELVET CAKE
1 eight-ounce package cream cheese, softened
1 box powdered sugar
Pinch of salt
1 teaspoon vanilla

Mix half the powdered sugar and salt with the cream cheese. Add the rest of the powdered sugar and vanilla; mix until smooth. Spread icing on cooled cake.

Every recipe I read for cream cheese icing calls for a stick of butter or margarine in addition to the cream cheese, but that makes the icing too thin for me. Possibly they mean a three-ounce package of cream cheese. Because of the fat content and the consistency of the icing, I prefer eight ounces of cream cheese and no butter or margarine.

CARROT CAKE IS S-O-O GOOD

Carrot cake is one of my favorites. My daughter says it is because I think the freshly grated carrots help redeem this cake, and they can't hurt. When I try to get my children to ask for carrot cake for their birthdays instead of Red Velvet, they remind me it doesn't have to be an occasion for me to bake them a cake.

Once when our family was camping my sister came to visit and brought a carrot cake. For days we had been eating only the kind of food that can be prepared on a temperamental gas stove, and I thought that was why the cake tasted so good. But since then I've decided this cake really is delicious, even when I haven't been out in the wilderness with no baked goods for several days.

CARROT CAKE

4 eggs
1½ cups vegetable oil
2 cups sugar
2 cups plain flour
1 teaspoon baking powder
1 teaspoon soda
2 teaspoons cinnamon
½ teaspoon salt
3 cups grated carrots

Blend eggs and oil, add sugar and mix. Sift flour and other dry ingredients. Add dry ingredients to egg mixture, mixing well. Add carrots; blend well. Pour mixture into two 9-inch cake pans lined with waxed paper. Bake at 375 degrees for 30 to 40 minutes.

ICING FOR CARROT CAKE
1 package (8 ounce) cream cheese, softened
1 stick butter, softened
1 box (16 ounce) powdered sugar
1½ teaspoons vanilla
1 cup pecans, chopped

Cream together cream cheese and butter. Add powdered sugar and vanilla, mixing well. Stir in nuts. Frost between layers, top and sides.

I have given you the original recipe. I adapt this cake by decreasing the oil to one cup. I decrease the cinnamon to one teaspoon because I don't want the overpowering flavor of cinnamon. I never use butter in the icing, just cream cheese.

ANOTHER FAVORITE—ITALIAN CREAM
This is the best cake (other than carrot) that I've ever tasted. It takes a little longer to make, but it is well worth the effort. Anytime a recipe calls for separated eggs, I beat the egg whites first. Always use either a glass or stainless steel bowl to beat egg whites; a plastic bowl doesn't work well. The recipes say to beat egg whites until stiff but not dry, or until soft peaks form. I've never figured out what that means, so I beat them until I can turn the bowl upside down and the beaten egg whites don't fall out.

ITALIAN CREAM CAKE
5 eggs, separated
1 stick butter or margarine, softened
½ cup shortening
2 cups sugar
1 teaspoon vanilla
2 cups plain flour
1 teaspoon soda
1 cup buttermilk
1 can angel-flake coconut
1 cup chopped nuts

Beat egg whites until stiff; set aside. Cream butter (or margarine) and shortening. Add sugar, egg yolks, and vanilla. Sift flour and soda together and add alternately to butter mixture with buttermilk. Add coconut, nuts, and vanilla. Fold in stiffly beaten egg whites. Bake in three eight or two nine inch cake pans for 25 to 30 minutes at 350 degrees.

ICING FOR ITALIAN CREAM CAKE
1 package (8 ounce) cream cheese
1 box powdered sugar
1 teaspoon vanilla
1 cup chopped nuts
Soften cream cheese. Add half the powdered sugar, mix well. Add the rest of the powdered sugar, vanilla and nuts. Beat until smooth, spread on cake.

SPELLING DOESN'T AFFECT
TASTE OF THIS CAKE
This recipe is in my handwritten cookbook as "Chocolate Sheath Cake," and my daughter copied it that way when she started her cookbook. Her husband has teased us unmercifully about that, because it is supposed to be sheet cake, baked in one layer, like a sheet. I tried to tell him that I found the recipe at the

same time sheath dresses, which had long, smooth lines, became popular, so that's where it got its name.

Whether "sheath" or "sheet," the cake is easy to make and a
chocolate lover's delight. You don't have to use a mixer and this
cake can be stirred up in a hurry.

CHOCOLATE SHEET CAKE
1 stick butter or margarine
½ cup shortening
4 tablespoons cocoa
1 cup of water
2 cups self-rising flour
2 cups sugar
½ cup buttermilk
2 eggs (well beaten)
1 teaspoon vanilla

Melt butter and shortening, add cocoa to make a paste, then
slowly add water. Bring mixture to a boil; remove from heat.
Stir flour and sugar together, add to butter mixture, mixing well.
Add buttermilk, beaten eggs and vanilla. Pour mixture into
greased rectangular 9 x 13 pan. Bake at 400 degrees 25 to 30
minutes.

ICING FOR CHOCOLATE SHEET CAKE
1 stick butter or margarine
4 tablespoons cocoa
6 tablespoons milk
1 box powdered sugar
1 teaspoon vanilla
1 cup chopped nuts

Start icing five minutes before cake is done. Melt butter,
add cocoa to make paste then slowly add milk. Bring mixture to
a boil; remove from heat and add powdered sugar, vanilla and
nuts, mixing well. Spread icing on cake while it is hot.

IF YOU LIKE APPLES,
YOU'LL LOVE THIS CAKE

I was introduced to this cake while spending a week with cousins. The seven of us savored this cake after every meal until it was gone. We served ourselves out of the baking pan, and one cousin kept apologizing for getting a few more bites, saying that she had to keep the edges straight. Soon it became the mission for all of us to keep the edges straight.

This cake is sinfully rich, but like the carrot cake, its redeeming factor is four cups of chopped apples. In fact, the hardest part of making this cake is chopping the apples, but it's well worth the effort. This is another cake that doesn't require a mixer.

APPLE DUMP CAKE
1 cup white raisins, plumped
4 cups chopped raw apples
2 cups sugar
½ cup oil
3 eggs, beaten
3 cups plain flour
2 teaspoons soda
1 teaspoon cinnamon
1 teaspoon cloves
¼ teaspoon salt
1 cup milk
2 teaspoons vanilla

Plump raisins by covering with boiling water; let stand. Drain before mixing in cake batter. Chop apples. Mix sugar and oil. Add eggs; mix well. Sift flour, soda, cinnamon, cloves and salt together. Add dry ingredients alternately with milk. Fold in vanilla, apples and raisins. Pour batter into greased 9 x 13 pan. Bake 45 minutes at 325 degrees.

ICING FOR APPLE DUMP CAKE
1 stick butter (softened)
1 (8 ounce) cream cheese (softened)
Dash salt
1 box powdered sugar
2 teaspoons vanilla

Cream butter and cream cheese. Add salt and half of the powdered sugar. Mix well. Add remaining powdered sugar. Add vanilla. Spread icing on warm cake. For a more moist cake, make holes in the cake with a toothpick after spreading the icing. Since this cake is frosted in the pan and the icing doesn't have to be thick enough to stay on layers, I do use the stick of butter in addition to the cream cheese.

If you don't like the taste of cloves, use two teaspoons cinnamon and omit the cloves. Low fat or fat free cream cheese works well in this recipe because the icing doesn't need to be thick. I've tried extra virgin olive oil in this cake and it works well. Use Granny Smith or other tart apples. Dark raisins will work just as well; white raisins look better.

EVERY COOK NEEDS A BASIC
POUND CAKE RECIPE
I know people who bake pound cakes and keep them in their freezer for emergencies. A pound cake is so versatile that it fits anywhere a dessert is needed. You can frost them or not as the mood strikes. A slice of pound cake can be covered with fruit and ice cream or whipped cream. Or it can be covered simply with ice cream. It can be eaten alone with a cup of coffee. I like to spread peanut butter on a slice of cake.

I think pound cake recipes must have started circulating about the time middle-class housewives began equipping their kitchens with electric or gas ranges. It was impossible to sustain even heat for the hour it took to cook a pound cake in the old wood stove, and kerosene ovens were too temperamental to risk baking a cake for that long. Below is the recipe for the first pound cake I ever made; it is still a treasured recipe.

POUND CAKE
1 cup shortening
2 cups sugar
4 eggs
1 teaspoon vanilla flavoring
1 teaspoon lemon flavoring
3 cups plain flour
1 teaspoon baking powder
1 teaspoon salt
1 cup milk

Cream together shortening and sugar. Add eggs one at a time. Add flavorings. Sift flour, baking powder and salt together. Add flour mixture alternately with milk to shortening/sugar mixture. Pour batter into well-greased tube pan and bake at 350 degrees one hour and 12 minutes. (I laughed when I saw directions for one hour and 12 minutes, but it worked perfectly for me.)

VARIATIONS ON POUND CAKE
To give the cake a different and delicious flavor, almond flavoring can be used instead of lemon.

To make a Butternut pound cake, add 2 tablespoons butternut flavoring to the above recipe and omit lemon flavoring.

To make an even better pound cake, substitute real butter for the shortening and cake flour for the plain flour.

The main difference in this recipe and the one above is that this one makes a larger cake.

BUTTER POUND CAKE
2 sticks butter or margarine, softened
½ cup shortening (Crisco)
3 cups sugar
6 eggs
1 teaspoon lemon
2 teaspoon vanilla
1 teaspoon almond
3 cups plain flour
½ teaspoon baking powder
½ teaspoon salt
1 cup evaporated milk

Cream butter, Crisco, and sugar. Add eggs, one at a time. Beat well. Add flavorings. Sift together flour, baking powder and salt. Add flour mixture to butter mixture alternately with milk. Bake in a well-greased tube cake pan at 350 degrees for one hour and 12 minutes.

CHOCOLATE POUND CAKE
½ cup shortening
½ cup butter or margarine, softened
3 cups sugar
5 eggs
1 teaspoon vanilla
5 tablespoons cocoa
3 cups flour
1 teaspoon baking powder
1 teaspoon salt
1 cup milk

Cream together shortening, butter and sugar. Add eggs, one at a time. Add vanilla. Sift together cocoa, flour, baking powder and salt. Add alternately with milk. Pour into well-greased tube pan and bake at 350 degrees for one hour and 12 minutes.

ICING FOR CHOCOLATE POUND CAKE
1 package (eight ounce) cream cheese
1 box powdered sugar
5 tablespoons cocoa
1 teaspoon vanilla
Pinch of salt

Soften cream cheese. Add ½ box powdered sugar. Mix well. Add other ingredients and continue mixing until icing is smooth. Spread on chocolate pound cake. If desired, place pecan halves around sides and on top of cake.

Once I took this cake to a picnic, intending to take the leftover cake home for my family to have for dessert over the weekend. There were no leftovers.

START THIS CAKE IN A COLD OVEN
IT REALLY WORKS
The next recipe is for a pound cake that literally melts in your mouth. In order for this to work in a cold oven, you need to have all the ingredients at room temperature before you start. I couldn't believe that a pound cake with no baking powder would rise, but this one does, and it is delicious. This cake doesn't need icing—in fact I think icing would take away from the flavor.

COLD OVEN POUND CAKE
2 sticks butter (no substitutions)
3 cups sugar
6 eggs
1 teaspoon vanilla
1 teaspoon almond
3 cups plain flour
½ pint whipping cream

Cream together butter and sugar. Add eggs one at a time. Add flavorings. Add heavy cream alternately with flour. Pour into greased tube pan. Start in cold oven. Bake at 325 degrees for one hour and 15 minutes.

MAKING A COCONUT CAKE WAS
QUITE AN ORDEAL FOR MAMA

People raved over Mama's coconut cake. And her cake should have received raves, not only because it was "melt-in-your-mouth-delicious," but also because making it was a major ordeal. The ordeal started when Mama bought a fresh coconut, which more times than not was sour. Because she didn't drive, she had to wait until someone could take the coconut back and exchange it for her. Since we lived only one block from town, this was not a problem when we were growing up. However, returning the soured coconut became increasingly more difficult after we started working and/or married and left home.

After Mama finally got a good coconut, she proceeded to crack it, usually with a hammer, or by throwing it down on concrete. Then came the tedious task of peeling the coconut, followed by the more tedious task of grating the coconut on the smallest side of the grater.

Then she made a three-layer cake from scratch. She made seven-minute frosting, which meant she stood by the stove, beating the frosting in a double boiler for at least seven minutes, with a rotary beater in the early days before she got an electric mixer.

She boiled the juice of the coconut with sugar, and used this liquid to moisten the cake--that's what made the cake so good. Then she put the cake together with the icing and coconut between each layer. She put coconut on the top and somehow managed to get the fresh grated coconut to stick to the sides of the cake. Mama's fresh coconut cake was a sight to behold and a delight to eat.

I never asked Mama for the recipe for her coconut cake because I never intend to spend that much time and effort on bak-

ing a cake, any cake. However, I found a recipe for an Easy Coconut Cake that is *almost* as good as Mama's.

EASY COCONUT CAKE
Bake a two-layer cake from a mix

EASY COCONUT CAKE ICING
16 ounces sour cream
2 cups sugar
2 (8 ounce) packages frozen coconut

The day before you bake the cake, mix the sour cream,
sugar and coconut; put in the refrigerator overnight. Bake a two-
layer cake. Slice the two layers in half, making four thin layers.
Spread icing between layers. Keep refrigerated.

The above recipe calls for a box of cake mix. You may get
energetic and want to bake a cake from scratch. The reason our
mothers and grandmothers cooked from scratch was that they
had to. To me, baking a cake from scratch is not that compli-
cated, and the results are well worth the effort.

TIPS ON BAKING A CAKE FROM SCRATCH
If the cake calls for separated eggs, it's a good idea to separate eggs in another container, adding egg whites to the mixing
bowl one at a time. The reason: if even a smidgen of the yellow
gets in the white, the white won't whip. Use that egg for something else. If you don't have an egg separator, they can be found
in stores that carry kitchen gadgets. Don't beat egg whites in a
plastic bowl; use either glass, ceramic or stainless steel.

I've never done the grease and flour cake pans business because I would get flour all over myself and my kitchen. Instead
I grease the edge of the pans then line the pans with waxed paper or parchment paper. I've even figured out a way to cut the
waxed paper with a minimum of fuss. I fold a piece of wax paper two or three times, depending on how many pans I'm using,
place one cake pan on the paper, trace the edge with the point of

my scissors, then cut wax paper liners for all cake pans at the same time.

Always preheat your oven before baking a cake except when a recipe specifically calls for starting in a cold oven.

Never peek to see how your cake is doing. Opening the oven will cause the cake to fall.

Listed below are four recipes for "scratch" cakes which are delicious and not too difficult to stir up. This one layer, one bowl cake couldn't be easier to make.

ONE BOWL CAKE
1½ cups plain flour
2½ teaspoons baking powder
½ teaspoon salt
¾ cup sugar
¾ cup milk
1/3 cup shortening
1 egg
1½ teaspoons vanilla

In a small mixer bowl combine all ingredients. (That's right. Put everything in the bowl in the order listed.) Beat with electric mixer until combined. Beat 2 minutes more on medium speed. Pour mixture into one prepared 9 inch round or square cake pan. Bake at 375 degrees 25 to 30 minutes.

I use this recipe to make a strawberry shortcake. I split the layers and put the strawberries on first then cover them with whipped cream. I use either real whipping cream, Cool Whip or Dream Whip. This cake will bring raves if you use fresh strawberries and real whipped cream.

This is your basic layer cake recipe if you want to make a "scratch" cake like your grandmother did.

YELLOW LAYER CAKE

½ cup shortening
1¾ cups sugar
1½ teaspoons vanilla
2 eggs
2¾ cups plain flour
2½ teaspoons baking powder
1 teaspoon salt
1¼ cups milk (not skim)

Beat shortening about 30 seconds. Add sugar and vanilla, mix well. Add eggs, one at a time, beating about one minute after each addition. Combine flour, baking powder and salt. Add dry ingredients and milk alternately to egg/shortening mixture, beating after each addition. Pour mixture into two 8 or 9 inch cake pans lined with waxed paper. Bake at 375 degrees 30 to 35 minutes.

ONE EGG CAKE RECIPE IS SIMPLE TO MAKE

This recipe is named One Egg Cake but I think it should also be called One Bowl because you just dump all the ingredients together and start mixing. The cake always turns out beautifully for me. If you don't want to measure the baking powder and salt, you can use self-rising flour. Use any type icing such as chocolate, caramel, lemon or coconut on this good, basic cake recipe.

ONE EGG CAKE
2 cups plain flour
1 1/3 cups sugar
2½ teaspoons baking powder
1 teaspoon salt
1/3 cup shortening
1 teaspoon vanilla
1 cup milk
1 egg

Mix dry ingredients in bowl. Add shortening, vanilla and 2/3 of milk. Beat 2 minutes at medium speed. Scrape sides and bottom of bowl constantly. Add remaining milk and egg. Beat 2 more minutes, scraping bowl frequently. Pour batter into two 8 or 9 inch cake pans lined with waxed paper. Bake at 350 degrees 25 to 30 minutes.

This two-egg chiffon cake takes a little longer to put together, but it, too, makes a beautiful cake which can be iced with any frosting you choose.

TWO EGG CHIFFON CAKE
2 eggs, separated
½ cup sugar
2 cups sugar
2¼ cups plain flour
3 teaspoons baking powder
1 teaspoon salt
1 cup milk

Beat egg whites until frothy. Gradually beat in ½ cup sugar. Continue beating until very stiff and glossy (or you can turn the bowl upside down). Mix remaining sugar, (2 cups), flour, baking powder and salt in another bowl. Add oil, flavoring, and half of milk. Beat at medium speed one minute. Scrape sides and bottom of bowl constantly. Add remaining milk and egg yolks. Beat one more minute, scraping bowl frequently. Fold in beaten egg whites. Bake in two 8 or 9 inch paper lined pans 30 to 35 minutes.

DON'T SHOOT THE COOK
SHE'S DOING THE BEST SHE CAN

I seldom ever make a cake from a mix, but I did try to make a spice cake from a mix for my granddaughter's third birthday. I don't know what happened to that cake, but all three layers split right down the middle. This cake couldn't be mended with toothpicks, though I tried. To make matters worse, I made a caramel icing that didn't get thick. I kept trying to put the icing back on the cake but it kept sliding off. It was a mess, pure and simple.

All the family, except Grandmother, had seen the cake, and they were talking and laughing about what a disaster it was. When Grandmother came in, she chided them for hurting my feelings. She said no matter how bad the cake looked, they shouldn't laugh at me because I had done my best.

Then she walked in the kitchen and saw the cake. Despite her efforts to control herself, she burst out laughing. It was a pitiful cake, but it didn't taste that bad, and we managed to eat it up without any trouble at all. Our granddaughter was too young to know how pitiful her birthday cake looked.

Since then I've found a caramel icing that does get thick, in fact it will get too thick if you cook it too long. I hesitate to include this recipe, because I always have trouble with it, but you may feel adventurous and want to try it. It must be named "No Fail" to bolster our courage.

NO FAIL CARAMEL ICING
1¼ sticks butter
6 tablespoons evaporated milk (or more)
2 cups brown sugar
½ teaspoon baking powder
1 teaspoon vanilla
1 box powdered sugar (or less)

Melt butter, add milk and brown sugar. Bring mixture to a boil and boil two minutes. Add baking powder and vanilla. Add powdered sugar and beat until smooth. Spread on cooled cake.

Don't boil the mixture any longer than two minutes. The last time I made this icing, the milk-sugar-butter mixture got too thick and I had a time spreading the icing on the cake.

(I saved this story for last because that's all it is--a story. I think you'll understand why after you've read it.)

I TRIED TO MAKE A FRUITCAKE ONCE--
ONCE WAS ENOUGH

Fruitcakes are not my favorites, so I waited a long time after I learned to cook before I ever tried to make one. I don't like the ingredients—peel and citron-- that give fruitcake a bitter taste. When I found what seemed to be the perfect recipe, I thought I'd give it a shot. This recipe called only for red and green cherries, pineapple and nuts. However, my biggest problem was that I didn't read the recipe carefully enough before I started mixing the cake.

One night after work I gathered all my ingredients and began. I've made all kinds of cakes: Carrot that calls for grated raw carrots. Red Velvet which says to mix vinegar and soda and watched it fizz. Italian Cream which requires a whole morning separating and beating eggs and chopping nuts. I've even made chocolate eclairs from scratch, so I didn't expect a fruitcake to defeat me.

Confidently I started mixing the cake. The family was downstairs watching television and I had my favorite music playing in the kitchen. I hummed along as I creamed the shortening and sugar, added egg yolks and flavoring. Sifted the flour with salt and baking powder. Coated the fruit with flour. Chopped the nuts and sliced the cherries and pineapple.

Then I got to the hard part. Beat egg whites until stiff but not dry. You've seen the directions. I don't know what dry is; I've never gotten egg whites to that stage. But even beating the egg whites didn't pose a problem. I finally learned, through experience, to use a glass or stainless steel bowl, not a plastic one, to beat egg whites. I don't know why, but egg whites just don't beat well in plastic.

By now I had my biggest mixing bowl full of flour, shortening, etc, and my next biggest bowl full of egg whites. Fold beaten egg whites into other mixture, the recipe said. There was no way. Both bowls were almost running over. Suddenly I understood why my mother used a dishpan to mix her fruitcake.

But my modern, dishwasher equipped kitchen didn't boast a dishpan.

What to do? What did I have big enough to mix the cake in? I thought of the top of my cake cover. I dumped the flour-fruit mixture in there and started trying to fold in the egg whites. Realizing I didn't have the strength to mix these two properly, I called my husband away from television to help me.

I was getting nervous, fearing the egg whites would fall before I could get them folded and all my effort--not to mention the cost of ingredients--would be lost. I handed him the big spoon and showed him how to fold the mixture.

He took the spoon and examined it. He found a miniscule spot of rust on it, then demanded to know why I was using a rusty spoon to mix the cake. He held it at an angle so he could see the rust better, and asked me to find something he could clean it with.

Rather than finding rust eradicator, I suggested that he forget the rust, and cleaning the spoon, and help me get the egg whites folded into the mixture before I had to throw the whole mess out. He wasn't too happy about using the less-than-perfect spoon, but he obliged.

I wish I could tell you the cake was a resounding success, that my family devoured it during the holidays, and that I have made a fruitcake every year since. But I can't. I excused their failure to eat the cake by saying we had too much other food. On several other occasions when I tried to get them to eat it, they were never "hungry for fruitcake." After the holidays, they were never hungry for fruitcake either, so I froze it.

That summer I took the fruitcake to our annual family beach vacation where there was a minimum of twenty family members in and out during the week. While relaxing at the beach we'll eat anything sweet and fattening—obviously anything sweet and fattening but fruitcake. My fruitcake held out to the very end. I was ready to throw it out, but after we finished cleaning the house and got everything packed and loaded, we finally ate the rest of it, simply because we were famished and there was nothing else left to eat.

As I'm sure you'll notice, a recipe doesn't follow this little outburst. I can't include the recipe because I threw it away long ago. Maybe you have a fruitcake recipe that is delicious and your family loves it. My advice is to use yours.

PIES

Pineapple Coconut Pie

Chocolate Pecan Pie

Pineapple Pie

Pie Cake

Fancy Pie Cake

Apple Pie Cake

Crustless Egg Custard

Crustless Coconut Custard

SOUTHERNERS ARE ALWAYS PREPARED
TO PROVIDE FOOD WHEN THERE'S A NEED

One summer's evening a woman from Up North was visiting Down South. The family relaxed on the front porch, luxuriating in the calmness and beauty of the landscape. Sitting on the porch with other family members was the grandmother of the family. Without so much as a final gasp, the grandmother quietly and peacefully died. The little old lady just dropped her gray head on her chest and silently left this world. As soon as word got out about Grandmother's demise, neighbors, friends, relatives and church folks started bringing in food to the bereaved family.

This Northern lady watched in awe as everyone rallied around the family. She had never even seen, much less tasted, so much good food in her life. When the family ran out of places to store food that couldn't be consumed immediately, neighbors volunteered their refrigerators and freezers.

So impressed was Miss Northern Lady that the day after the funeral, she got on the phone, called a realtor, and instructed him to find her a house in that neighborhood. What Miss Northern Lady didn't know was that she could have bought a house in any established Southern neighborhood, or joined any local church, and she would have been treated just as royally.

We Southerners do love to cook and to eat, and we tend to show our love, concern and sympathy with food. From the time news spreads about the death until the last meal after the funeral, people are constantly in and out of the house designated for the family, and mealtime rolls around regularly. The better known or loved the deceased, the more food brought in. And not just any kind of food. Homemakers pull out their prize recipes and deliver the food in their best dishes, with an address label on the bottom of the dish so it can be returned. However, we have moved slightly into the twenty-first century now and to lessen the burden on the family, often we take food in disposable dishes

Any Southern woman worth her salt will have something in her freezer she can pull out and send to the family in an emergency. If she happens to be caught short because she just sent that pound cake to Cousin Minnie's family last week, she can always make sandwiches or whip up a dessert in a hurry. For this reason we have recipes that can be made in a short time, but taste as if you slaved half a day. Listed below are four of my favorites that fit this category.

PINEAPPLE COCONUT PIES
1 stick butter or margarine
2 cups sugar
4 eggs
1 can (10 ½ ounce) angel flake coconut
1 can (8 ounce) crushed pineapple
2 nine-inch pie shells

Cream margarine or butter with sugar. Beat eggs separately then combine with creamed mixture. Add pineapple and coconut. Pour into unbaked pie shells. Bake at 350 degrees for 35 to 40 minutes. Use regular pie shells. Deep-dish shells aren't necessary; they make the ingredients look skimpy and we certainly don't want that.

CHOCOLATE PECAN PIES
1 stick butter or margarine, melted
2 cups sugar
7 tablespoons cocoa
3 eggs
1 1/3 cups evaporated milk
1 cup chopped pecans
Two nine-inch pie shells

Cream butter or margarine with sugar and cocoa. Beat eggs separately and add to creamed mixture. Slowly beat in evaporated milk. Stir in pecans. Pour mixture into two unbaked pie shells. Bake at 350 degrees for 30 minutes.

You can use deep-dish shells if you want because this mixture is very thin. These pies need to be chilled for several hours or overnight before slicing.

PINEAPPLE PIE
1 large container Cool Whip
1 can (8 ounce) crushed pineapple, drained
3 tablespoons lemon juice
1 can (15 ounce) Eagle brand milk
(sweetened condensed)
1 cup chopped pecans

Mix ingredients and place in two cooked pie shells, or two graham cracker shells. Store in freezer until serving time

PIE CAKE
1 can (16 ounce) fruit
1 stick butter or margarine
1 box (8 ounce) yellow cake mix (Jiffy)

Place fruit* in a one quart casserole. Spread cake mix over fruit. Cut one stick butter or margarine in approximately 16 pieces and cover cake mix. Bake at 375 degrees for 35 to 40 minutes. Serve warm, topped with ice cream or frozen yogurt.

*You can use canned or frozen cherries, blackberries, blueberries, peaches, strawberries, or any fresh fruit you have on hand. We like tart cherries with no sugar added and we prefer cans of fruit packed in their own juice instead of fruit pie filling. Chopped pecans are good added to apple pies and slivered almonds on peach pies.

FANCY PIE CAKE
1 can (15 ½ ounce) cherries
1 can (8 ounce) crushed pineapple
1 box (8 ounce) cake mix (Jiffy)
1 stick butter or margarine
1 cup chopped pecans

Layer ingredients in order listed. Bake at 375 degrees for 35 to 40 minutes.

APPLE PIE CAKE
4 to 6 medium sized Granny Smith apples, sliced
¼ cup water
¼ cup sugar
1 teaspoon cloves
1 box (8 ounce) cake mix (Jiffy)
1 stick butter or margarine

Layer apples in casserole dish. Cover with water. Mix sugar and cloves, sprinkle over apples. Spread cake mix over apples. Slice butter or margarine over cake mix. Bake at 375 degrees 35 to 40 minutes.

You can reduce the amount of sugar and/or cloves, or substitute cinnamon for cloves. You may want to add more water. Because I like more fruit in my pie, I love to fill my dish almost to overflowing with sliced apples. Recently I made a pie for a crowd and I used a three-pound bag of apples, two boxes of cake mix, and two sticks of butter.

HEALTH TIPS: None. All of these desserts are loaded with fat and sugar, but everyone needs to cheat occasionally. However, I have discovered that you can use less butter on the pie cake by putting thinner slices over the cake mix.

These two custard recipes don't have piecrusts, and only one-fourth stick of butter each, so at least you won't be putting hydrogenated shortening in your body when you eat these custards.

CRUSTLESS EGG CUSTARD
¼ stick butter
2 tablespoons flour
3 eggs
½ cup sugar
1 tall can evaporated milk
1 teaspoon vanilla

Melt butter in pie pan. Stir in flour until smooth. In another bowl beat eggs; slowly add sugar, evaporated milk and vanilla. Pour mixture in pie pan. Bake at 350 degrees for 30 to 40 minutes.

CRUSTLESS COCONUT CUSTARD
½ cup flour
1½ cups sugar
4 eggs
1 cup evaporated milk
1 cup whole milk
¼ stick butter, melted
1 teaspoon vanilla
1 (7 ounce) package flaked coconut

Sift flour and sugar together. Beat eggs, evaporated milk, whole milk and vanilla. Add melted butter. Combine egg mixture with flour and sugar mixture. Fold in coconut. Pour into greased nine-inch pie plate. Bake at 350 degrees for 50 minutes.

COOKIES/DESSERTS

Naomi's Bread Pudding

Cornelia's Banana Pudding

Marie's Dessert

Applesauce Oatmeal Cookies

Golden Lemon Bars

Brownies

Congo Bars

Refrigerator Cookies

Oatmeal Drop Cookies

Rice Krispie Treats

NAOMI'S BREAD PUDDING
1 stick butter
2 loaves French bread
6 eggs
3 tablespoons brown sugar
¾ cup white sugar
1 teaspoon cinnamon
2 teaspoons vanilla flavoring
2 quarts whole milk
2 ounces Rum
½ cup raisins

Melt butter in large pan. Fill pan with crumbled bread. Beat eggs, add sugars and flavorings. Slowly beat in milk. Add Rum and raisins. Pour mixture over bread. Let soak a few hours or overnight. Bake at 350 degrees for 45 minutes.

oNAOMIo

SAUCE
1 stick butter
¾ cup sugar
½ cup water
2 ounces rum

In a saucepan, melt butter; add sugar, water and rum. Bring to a boil. You can pour this sauce over the entire pudding, but I think it's best to spoon it on individual servings. Be sure to serve it warm.

° CORNELIA °

CORNELIA'S BANANA PUDDING
One package (3½ ounce) vanilla instant pudding
2 cups milk
1 container (8 ounce) sour cream
Vanilla wafers
Bananas (about four)

Mix one package instant pudding with two cups milk according to directions. Let the pudding set just a few minutes until it begins to thicken. Fold in an eight-ounce container of sour cream. Put a layer of vanilla wafers in bowl. Slice bananas on the wafers. Alternate pudding with wafers and bananas. Use a minimum amount of wafers and bananas so there's lots and lots of creamy pudding.

A friend introduced me to this dessert; it has a name I've long since forgotten so we simply call it Marie's Dessert. When I took it to a neighborhood picnic, I knew everyone would want the recipe, so I took it in my pocket. The interesting thing about this dish is that everyone thinks it has bananas in it.

If you're so inclined, you could use cooked pudding, or make the pudding from scratch, but instant pudding works just as well. The only reason I have found for not using instant is that instant pudding tends to separate after a day or so. But you won't have that problem with this dessert; nothing will be left in a day or so.

You can put the finished product into two small bowls, keep one for your family and share the other. The dessert looks beautiful in a large glass bowl.

MARIE'S DESSERT
One (13 ounce) angel food cake
2 packages (3 ½ ounce) instant vanilla pudding
4 cups milk
1 can (8 ounce) crushed pineapple
1 container (13 ounce) Cool Whip
1 can (3 ½ ounce) angel flake coconut

Break cake into bite-sized pieces, place in large bowl. Mix two boxes of instant vanilla pudding according to package directions. Stir pineapple into pudding. Pour mixture over cake pieces; mixing so that pudding covers all the cake. Spread Cool Whip over the top, sprinkle with coconut. To make this dessert even more festive, add a few well-drained red maraschino cherries on top of the coconut.

While our daughter was in college, I tried to find a "goody" for her that was both tasty, nutritious and easy to store in a dorm room. I found this recipe, which calls not only for oatmeal, but also for raisins and applesauce. When she was a freshman, she came home almost every weekend and I made these cookies for her to take back to munch on.

APPLESAUCE OATMEAL COOKIES
¾ cup shortening
1 cup firmly packed brown sugar
1 egg
2 cups sifted all-purpose flour
½ teaspoon baking soda
½ teaspoon salt
½ teaspoon cinnamon
½ teaspoon nutmeg
1½ cups uncooked rolled oats (quick or old-fashioned)
½ cup raisins
1 cup applesauce

Cream shortening and brown sugar. Add egg and mix well. Sift flour, baking soda, salt and spices, add to shortening mix. Add rolled oats, raisins and applesauce and mix well. Drop by tablespoonfuls on greased cookie sheet. Bake at 350 degrees for 12 to 15 minutes. Makes about 3 dozen.

Since I love the taste of cloves with apples and don't like nutmeg, I substitute cloves for the nutmeg. You could also add ½ cup nuts and make these cookies even more nutritious.

I found this recipe on the back of a brown sugar box, and it says it is a world famous recipe. I always glance at recipes on boxes and cans, and I've found several good recipes that way. In fact this recipe is so good that I don't change a thing when I make these bars. My only warning is that they are so rich that you can eat only a small amount at a time, but that just makes them last longer. This recipe comes in three parts, so be sure to read the entire recipe before you start.

GOLDEN LEMON BARS

CRUST
1 stick (softened) butter or margarine
½ cup brown sugar
1½ cups flour
Combine soft butter, brown sugar and flour and pat into 9 x 13 pan (which doesn't have to be greased because of the amount of butter.) Bake 10 minutes at 275 degrees

FILLING
2 eggs, well beaten
2 tablespoons flour
½ teaspoon baking powder
¼ teaspoon salt
½ teaspoon vanilla
1 cup brown sugar
1¼ cups coconut
½ cup chopped pecans

Beat eggs. Add flour, baking powder, salt and vanilla. Mix with brown sugar. Add coconut and pecans. Pour mixture over baked pastry. Bake an additional 20 minutes at 350 degrees

GLAZE
1 tablespoon butter, melted
2 tablespoon lemon juice
1 cup powdered sugar

Mix butter, lemon juice and powdered sugar. Pour glaze over baked bars in pan. Let cool and slice into squares.

I had a problem finding a brownie recipe that suited me. My cookbook had a recipe for cake brownies--which were too much like cake, and chewy brownies--which were too much like candy, so I combined these recipes and came up with the one listed below.

I published this recipe in a column I was writing at the time in the local newspaper. Years later a friend of a friend called and asked me for the recipe. Seems she had tried it, and liked it, but had lost her copy. I was thrilled to share the recipe with her and pleased to know that it had become part of her collection.

Since this recipe makes 32 or 50 brownies, depending on how you cut them, you feel as if your effort has been worthwhile. If you want to make these brownies special, frost with chocolate frosting and place a pecan half on each one.

MY ORIGINAL BROWNIE RECIPE
1 stick butter or margarine, softened
½ cup shortening
1 cup sugar
4 eggs
1 teaspoon vanilla
5 tablespoons cocoa
1¼ cups plain flour

½ teaspoon baking powder
½ teaspoon salt
1 cup chopped nuts

Cream together butter and shortening. Add sugar. Add eggs, one at a time. Add vanilla. Sift together cocoa, flour, baking, powder and salt. Add to creamed mixture. Stir in nuts.

Bake in two eight-inch square pans at 350 degrees for 30 minutes. I grease the sides and put waxed paper in the bottom. If you try to cook this recipe in one large pan, the brownies will get hard around the edges and the middle will be undercooked. Two pans works much better.

A good companion recipe to brownies is Congo Bars. Children and teenagers love both brownies and Congo Bars. These recipes, both made in two eight-inch square pans, will go quite a way in serving a group of people, so if you have to serve refreshments to a bunch of hungry kids, or teenagers, why not try these recipes? By the way, adults like them, too.

CONGO BARS
2/3 cup shortening, melted and cooled
1 box (16 ounce) light brown sugar.
3 eggs
1 teaspoon vanilla
2¾ cups plain flour
2½ teaspoons baking powder
½ teaspoon salt
1 cup chopped nuts
1 package (8 ounce) chocolate chips

Mix melted, cooled shortening with brown sugar. Add eggs, one at a time. Add vanilla. Sift together flour, baking powder, and salt. Add to creamed mixture. At this point you will probably have to set aside your mixer and continue mixing by hand as this batter is very stiff. Add nuts and chocolate chips. Bake in two eight-inch square pans lined with wax paper at 350 degrees for 25 to 30 minutes. DO NOT bake in one large pan.

This batter is so stiff that you may not be able to spread it to the edges of the pan. Don't worry. It will spread as it cooks. Do not overcook or bars will be hard. Because of laziness, I've often used oil with this recipe but I think the shortening works best. I've substituted both peanut butter chips and butterscotch chips with good results. Some cooks leave out the chocolate chips or the nuts or both, but I love these bars chock full of chocolate chips and nuts.

FRESH FROM THE OVEN COOKIES

One of my most pleasant memories is coming home from school to find a dishpan full of homebaked sugar cookies, the kind you roll and cut. Mama didn't make these cookies very often, but when she did you can imagine the pleasure we children had eating them with a glass of cold milk.

I've read that children who enjoy home baked goodies in their house don't experiment with drugs. I don't know if there's any statistical evidence to back up this statement, but I didn't take any chances. Since I love to cook I always had something sweet at our house while our children were growing up. As soon as we ate up the current dessert, I made another. I have never been able to master the roll and slice cookie, but I found another recipe that tastes just as good and is not nearly as hard to make.

REFRIGERATOR COOKIES

1/3 cup shortening, softened
½ cup butter
½ cup granulated sugar
½ cup brown sugar
1 egg
1 teaspoon vanilla
2 cups plain flour

1 teaspoon baking powder
½ teaspoon salt
½ cup chopped pecans

Cream together shortening, butter, and sugars. Add egg and vanilla. Sift flour, baking powder and salt. Add to mixture and mix well. Add nuts. Shape dough into a roll and wrap. Chill thoroughly. Cut dough in slices and bake at 425 degrees for 5 to 7 minutes. You can slice this dough paper-thin and have wafer-like cookies or slice it thicker for chewy cookies. Experiment and find which you like best.

TWO RECIPES CHILDREN LOVE
My boys loved this oatmeal cookie, which has nothing nutritious about it except the oatmeal and the peanut butter. What this recipe has going for it is its simplicity. They look and taste more like candy than cookies, which is part of their appeal.

If it's the day before grocery day and there's no junk food left in the house, the kids are wailing "What can I eat?" and you don't have time to stir up any goodies, let them make these Oatmeal Drop Cookies for themselves.

OATMEAL DROP COOKIES
1 stick butter or margarine
2 cups sugar
¼ cup cocoa
½ cup milk
2 cups (quick cooking) oatmeal
1 teaspoon vanilla
1 heaping tablespoon peanut butter

Melt butter or margarine in a heavy, two-quart saucepan. Mix sugar and cocoa together, add to butter. Add milk. Bring mixture to a rolling boil, boil 2 minutes. Remove from heat; add oatmeal and peanut butter. (Crunchy peanut butter is even better.) Mix well. Drop by heaping teaspoonfuls on waxed paper. These cookies are ready to eat as soon as they cool.

RICE KRISPIE TREATS
1 cup sugar
1 cup (Karo maple) syrup
1 jar (12 ounce) crunchy peanut butter
5 to 6 cups Rice Krispies

Mix sugar and syrup to boiling. Let boil 30 seconds. Stir in peanut butter. Add Rice Krispies. Press into Pyrex dish or pan and cut into squares.

That's all, folks.

In addition to this cookbook and the play, *The Proof Is in the Pudding*, Evelyn Nalley McCollum has published a family history, *Nalley, A Southern Family Story*. She has worked as a journalist and freelance writer, publishing both fiction and nonfiction in regional and religious magazines and has won writing awards. After writing a column for *The Easley Progress* over ten years, she compiled these columns in four books, *Just Between You and Me*. She entered college at age fifty and earned a BA in history from Clemson University with a minor in religion. Her hobbies, in addition to writing and cooking, are gardening, reading and spending time with family and friends. She and her husband Marion live in Easley, South Carolina. They have three children and eight grandchildren.

Evelyn

Claire

Claire Gray Zeigler, granddaughter of Marion and Evelyn McCollum and daughter of Ed and Susan Zeigler, graduated from Greenville High School. She then studied at Savannah College of Art and Design in Georgia, where she earned a BFA in Interior Design in 2007. She currently resides in Charlotte, NC where she is employed by Anthropologie.

SUBJECT INDEX

Oven Baked Tenderloin.....32
Parmesan Chicken Fingers.....31
Salmon-Crabmeat Patties.....38
Salmon Croquettes.....37
Tuna Casserole.....35

PIES
Apple Pie Cake.....107
Chocolate Pecan Pie.....105
Crustless Coconut Custard.....108
Crustless Egg Custard.....108
Fancy Pie Cake.....115
Pie Cake.....107
Pineapple Coconut Pie.....105
Pineapple Pie.....106

SALADS
Annabel's Prized Jell-O Salad.....12
Bean Salad with Artichoke Hearts.....7
Black Bean Salad.....6
Black Bean Pasta Salad.....6
Black-eyed Pea Salad......9
Broccoli Cauliflower Salad.....10
Chicken or Turkey Salad.....5
Chicken Salad.....4
Corn and Pea Salad....8
Fruit Salad.....11
Fruited Chicken Salad.....4
Holiday Turkey Salad.....5
Jell-O Salads.....13
Salmon Salad.....3
Sauer Kraut Salad....9
Seven Layer Salad.....11
Tuna Salad......3
Turkey Salad......5
White Bean and Tuna Salad......8

SOUPS
Brown Rice and Lentil Soup.....24
Chili and Beans.....25

STORIES

ALPHABETICAL INDEX

Y

ORDER BLANK

The Proof is in the Pudding Cookbook
Evelyn McCollum
409 Haverhill Circle
Easley SC 29642

Please send me _____ autographed copies of *The Proof Is in the Pudding Cookbook* at $10.95 each, postage paid in the United States.

Name: _____

Address: _____

City, State and Zipcode:_____

1-864-859-5239
Evegray854@charter.net

- -

The Proof is in the Pudding Cookbook
Evelyn McCollum
409 Haverhill Circle
Easley SC 29642

Please send me _____ autographed copies of *The Proof Is in the Pudding Cookbook* at $10.95 each, postage paid in the United States.

Name: _____

Address: _____

City, State and Zipcode:_____

1-864-859-5239
Evegray854@charter.net

www.ingramcontent.com/pod-product-compliance
Lightning Source LLC
Chambersburg PA
CBHW030108070426
42448CB00036B/480